# Winners Make It Happen
## Reflections of a Self-Made Man

By Leonard H. Lavin

*Founding President, C.E.O. and
Chairman of the Alberto-Culver Company*

With Daniel Paisner

Chicago and Los Angeles

07 06 05 04 03    5 4 3 2 1

Lavin, Leonard H.
    Winners make it happen: reflections of a self-made man/by Leonard H.
Lavin with Daniel Paisner.
    p. cm.
Includes index.
    ISBN 1-56625-206-7
    1. Lavin, Leonard H.    2. Businessmen—United States—Bibliography
    3. Alberto-Culver Co.—History.
    4. Toilet preparations—United States—History.
I. Paisner, Daniel.    II. Title.

Bonus Books
875 N. Michigan Ave., Ste. 1416
Chicago, IL 60611

Printed in the United States of America

Winners make it happen; losers let it happen.

—Leonard Lavin

# Contents

# Introduction

I FEEL AS THOUGH I SHOULD BEGIN THIS BOOK BY DECLARING WHAT IT is I am not, before I state who I am or what I've done or how I've reached whatever level of success upon which I now stand. Humility, I've often thought, is one of the most underappreciated virtues, which, I suppose, explains why it is also one of the least apparent. Those who know me might suggest that I've never been one to boast of my accomplishments or wear them on my sleeve. This much, I hope, will become clear as you read these pages. Of course, there is a certain amount of unavoidable bluster in a project such as this—after all, I can't expect to write about my life, business dealings, and other not-so-trivial pursuits and *not* to mention any of the triumphs along the way. So I'll attempt to present these clearly, and without agenda, because what's interesting to me is not each and every triumph itself, but how each positive step took me to the next one, and the one after that, and so on. I also find it interesting that the occasional misstep has sometimes redirected me toward an unanticipated goal, and I will seek to highlight these as well, with notes and comments.

And so, at the outset, I will follow my instincts, which, as you'll also see as you read along, is a course that's served me well. Therefore, read what I am not.

I am not a flashy tycoon.

I am not a business-schooled or (fully) college-educated entrepreneur.

I am not a strategist.

I am not a student of corporate management theories or motivational techniques.

I am not the sort of leader who is arrogant, full of himself, or otherwise considers himself beyond reproach.

I am not an empire builder.

I am not a galvanizing, proselytizing, aggrandizing, or otherwise "-izing" presence on the American business scene.

I am not a darling of Wall Street analysts—although I should point out that a small investment in our company's stock, when first issued in 1961, would have realized a 5,200 percent rate of return over the next forty years.

I am not a household name—except, perhaps, in my own (although, even at home, there have been times I couldn't get a hearing)—and I haven't spent my career reinventing any wheels, building any better mousetraps, or discovering any cures for any ills.

And finally, I am not a genius by any stretch, although I will boast that I have a pretty good knack for recognizing a good idea or product and figuring out a way to bring that good idea or product to the marketplace. There is no genius in this, only instinct. And there is no secret to it, either, for if there were, I'd be happy to share it, and then we'd all be successful. I go by my gut, and over the past fifty or so years, my gut has taken me to some pretty interesting places.

This, I suppose, brings me full circle back to what I am: I am, simply, a good marketing person, a salesman, a business manager, and a straight-shooter. In the course of my colorful career, I've managed to develop and market a line of hair care and other household products that now can be found in virtually every other home in America and in millions more around the world. I've done this without the benefit of any formal business education and without any start-up funds, limited partnerships, or serious financial backing. And I've done these things in the shadows of some real corporate giants, in the kind of closely held family business environment that seems to have left our economic landscape.

I set out to make a living, and, in the process, built a brand—indeed, a shelf—full of worldwide brands.

I commit these words to paper now because more and more I find myself looking over my shoulder at the life I've lived, at some of the business decisions I've made, and at the compelling crossroads I still must consider. You see, I'm eighty-two years old, and I can't do these kinds of things forever. It's taken me a while to come to this realization, but I have come to it. Now that I'm here, I mean to set down for the record how it is I got here, what I meant to do on arrival, what I've managed to do instead, and what I plan to do going forward. I've also begun to think that somewhere in the arc of my life and career lies a blueprint for a new generation of entrepreneurs. After all, there are no new tricks in our new economy, only new men and women at the helm.

"Winners make it happen," goes the company credo I coined back when we were just starting out. "Losers let it happen."

Words to live by, wouldn't you agree? I've certainly sought to pattern my life after them, and I've encouraged do the same.

What follows is an account and a reflection, a thorough going-over of the path to my present position as the founding president, CEO and, still, chairman of a Fortune 500 Company—a company I birthed and of which I am very proud. Along that path, I trust that you will rediscover with me what it takes to *make* things happen.

# 1

## The Spirit of Enterprise

I WAS BORN ON OCTOBER 29, 1919, AND FOR MY TENTH BIRTHDAY, THE
stock market crashed. It is one of the most indelible memories
of my childhood—as it was for virtually every child of my generation—but in my case, it was more of a backdrop than a defining
moment. See, in our house, we always had enough to eat. We wore
decent, respectable clothing. We lived comfortably. We were never
rich, mind you, not by any stretch, but the Depression hit other
Chicago families a lot harder than it hit ours. Don't misunder-
stand me, the hard times *did* find us, but only on occasion—and
on those occasions, things were never too terribly hard.

My father, Samuel Lavin, grew up on a farm in Michigan—a
childhood about as far removed from my own urban upbringing
as you can imagine. Most everyone on my father's side of the family was in the flower business, so I always assumed they grew flowers on the farm, but, in truth, I never knew what kind of farm it
was. What did I know? I was a city boy who lived for the present,
with no curiosity for the past, and my father was a striving, young
businessman anxious to make his own mark. He never talked
about it, and I never thought to ask. That was how it was with a
lot of families back then. Your past was your past, and your future was wide open. What counted was the present, and my father
lived smack in the middle of the present. My mother called him
the original Communist for the way he built up businesses and

then handed them back to his employees. He did this three or four times, by my mother's count, which, in her estimation, was about three or four times too many. I don't know if this was part of some grand philosophy my father had to share the wealth, if he was just a good guy, or maybe if he was just a bad business-man, but from my mother's lips, the stories of my father's adventures were legendary. He started one of Chicago's first public taxi services just after World War I, but he was long out of it by the time it grew into the profitable fleet of the Yellow Cab Company. Later on, he made a decent living as a gently used appliance salesman. He got his hands on old vacuum cleaners for a dollar or two, then he had the handles painted, put new bags on the things, maybe fixed the motors or polished the chrome, or did whatever else needed to be done. Then he went out to one of the small towns outside the city and sold them for twenty-five dollars or so. He made a nice profit on each machine and sold maybe half a dozen a day. He expanded these efforts until he was able to open a store, and soon after that, a small chain of stores, but eventually he grew tired of this as well. To hear my mother tell it, he just gave the stores away, but what seems more likely is that he gave equity to people who helped him out. Ten percent here, 10 percent there . . . after a while, it added up until there was nothing left, and this seemed to coincide with my father losing any personal interest in the business as well.

Sporting events were about the only area of sustaining interest in my father's world. Sports and gambling, in those days, appeared to go hand in hand—at least that's the way they appeared to me in my limited world view. My father was an avid Detroit Tigers fan, but, living in Chicago, he came to root for the Cubs and the White Sox as well. He just loved baseball, and he passed that love down to me. In fact, he loved all sports, and, soon enough, so did I. He took me to the Dempsey-Tunney fight at Soldier Field when I was six or seven years old. I still can remember the bustle, hoopla, and raw excitement of the place; every time I've been to the fights since, it's paled by comparison, and every time I've stepped into that hallowed stadium, I've been taken back to that first visit, all those years ago. And he took the whole family to Churchill Downs for my first Kentucky Derby. I rooted for the winner in that first Derby. It was 1928, and we were guests of John D. Hertz, a friend of my father's, who happened to own the winning horse, Reigh Count. I didn't know much about handicapping in those days—honestly, I didn't know the first thing!—but I smartly figured that if we were guests of one of the owners, I would do well to bet on the man's horse, so I did. Reigh Count won the race, and I was hooked. I was eight years old, and I haven't missed many Derbies since. Here again, each visit has been measured against the very first.

Indeed, my father's twin passions for sports and gambling took me directly to my first lesson in making money or building a business: never bet on anyone but yourself. A simple lesson, to be sure, and a basic truth, but I came upon it in a sidelong way. My father's oldest brother, Jack, was what they used to call a commission man. He took bets that were too big for most other bookies to hold—on horse races, fights, and ball games—and then laid them off with other bookmakers in other parts of the country. He had his counterparts in such cities as New York, St. Louis, and Philadelphia, and, in each city, there was someone willing to take the action. Uncle Jack made his money on the 5 or 10 percent commission and didn't much care who won the bet. It was a good business, even if it was a shade unseemly. My father threw in with his brother during the depths of the Depression, and, for a while, they made an awful lot of money. It was an awful lot of money during such hard times, but it was also an awful lot of money, period. For me, it was a great treat, this time in my father's life, because it opened all kinds of doors to a wide-eyed fan like me. I was just a kid, ten or twelve years old, and I was going to ball games, developing a taste for thoroughbreds, and sitting in the bleachers with all kinds of gamblers and scoundrels. It was wonderful. I wouldn't have traded that particular piece of my childhood for anything.

One summer afternoon in 1932, I came home, and my mother greeted me at the door with a message from my father. He wanted me to get into a cab and meet him downtown at his office in the Wrigley Building, whereupon we would continue to the ballpark to see the Cubs. This, alone, was not unusual. We took in a lot of games together, often on the spur of the moment. On this visit, though, my father came out of the office to meet me when I arrived. There was something firm in his manner, something serious. "Now look," he said. "I'm going to take you into your uncle's office. Don't say a word. Just say hello. No matter what you see in there, I don't want you to say anything, understand?"

I nodded that I understood, and we went inside. Realize, at this time, my uncle's operation was fairly elaborate. There were dozens of people on the telephone, switchboard operators, and people accepting bets from all over the country and laying off the action wherever they could find a taker. It was a real boiler-room setup, and I walked with my father past all the bustle and excitement toward my uncle's office, not really thinking of my father's warning. I'd been up here before and seen all this action. It was always exciting, but it was nothing new.

Just then, we opened the door to my uncle's office, and my eyes nearly popped out of my head. There was Uncle Jack, sitting across from one of the great ballplayers of the era. There was no such thing as the Hall of Fame at the time, but this man surely fit the bill, and I won't offer his name here because I don't want to sully his otherwise fine reputation. I don't know if it was a regular habit of this man's to consort with a commission man like my uncle, or if it was just a one-time deviation. Even these many years later, I feel honor-bound to protect his identity sufficiently enough still to tell the story. The story, I feel, is important for the lesson it holds, but not so important that it should dampen a great man's reputation. You never know why a man does an unethical

thing once, and you can only imagine why he might make a habit
of it.

I started to say something, but before I could open my mouth,
my father grabbed me by the arm and squeezed so hard that I
swear I sometimes still can see his fingerprints there. I stood
silently and listened, and what I could make out was that the
famous ballplayer was wagering two thousand dollars. And—I
couldn't believe my ears—he was betting against his own team!
Naturally, this was some time after the notorious Black Sox scan-
dal, when members of the Chicago White Sox were alleged to have
thrown the World Series to collect on a bet. That happened the
year I was born. This sort of thing supposedly didn't happen any
more—goodness, it wasn't supposed to have happened in 1919!—
which was why I was fairly incredulous as I stood there on the
perimeter of the scene. Here was a man I rooted for, betting
against the team I rooted for, with the kind of wager most Americans then would have considered a respectable salary. It was astonishing. I was old enough to understand what it all meant and
to consider the various ramifications, but I kept quiet.

The future Hall of Famer finished his business with my uncle,
then he stood, shook hands, and made to leave. After that, my father tidied up a few things around the office and took me out to
Wrigley Field to see the ball game. This had been his plan all
along. The Cubs, who finished in first place in the National
League that season, were playing the Cardinals, who finished next
to last. The Cubs had a tall righthander in his first full season,
and he was scheduled to pitch; the great Dizzy Dean, also in his
first full season, was going for the Cardinals. The game turned
out to be a real pitchers' duel, and I actually forgot about the
wager in my uncle's office during the middle innings. It was, in
every respect, a hard-fought contest, just the sort of thing a ball-
game should be. There was nothing on the field to arouse any sort
of suspicion, so I put what I had seen in my uncle's office happily out of mind—until the sixth inning, when the Cubs's rookie
pitcher was lifted for a pinch hitter. Of course, nowadays, it's

nothing to pull a pitcher early, especially to capitalize on a scoring opportunity in a tight game, but the convention in those days was for a pitcher to go the distance unless he was really getting shellacked. And that was just the thing: the rookie had pitched a great game, but he was taken out, and the Cubs still were unable to push anything across against Dean. In his place, the Cubs brought in some bum who got lit up in the later innings, and the Cardinals wound up winning the game in lopsided fashion.

My uncle's client—an icon of the game!—won his bet, and I learned a hard lesson: never bet on professional sports. My father wasn't much of a talker and expected the events of the day to speak for themselves without explanation, but, on the ride home, he did offer this: "These athletes, you can't trust 'em any further than you can throw 'em."

I took his advice to heart, and to this day, I've never bet on a professional sporting contest. I'll bet on the horses, which is something I've come to know a good deal about, although, even with racing, you never can be sure if a horse is out to win a race or just out to build experience. But horses don't cheat. It's the human element you have to worry about, and I've expanded my father's warning to include any business dealing out of my immediate control. If I can't see a situation fully, understand it from all angles, and eliminate as many uncertainties as possible, I'll leave the opportunity for someone else. As I learned that afternoon in 1932, my pockets will never be deep enough to gamble on the whims of others.

It's a lesson I've done well to follow, although it was a helluva way to have to learn it.

My mother, Ella, didn't much care for sports. She cared even less for the commission business, and, soon enough, my father was out of that and onto some new scheme. She held a lot of sway in our household, my mother did, which, I suppose, is how it was in a lot of Jewish homes in Chicago during the Depression. She came from an Orthodox family, and she came to believe that no Jewish man should be in the gambling business. My father went along with her. He went along with her on a lot of things. He was not raised to be a particularly observant Jew, but my mother kept a kosher home. That is, she kept kosher as long as there was no good reason not to do so. When my sister Gloria had an operation on her ear as a young child, and the doctor reported that bacon fat was about the best thing to help speed her recovery, my mother went out and bought up all the bacon in the neighborhood.

We observed the Sabbath when it was convenient. We went to synagogue when it was convenient. I even went to Hebrew school from time to time—usually when I couldn't get around it. I was a fairly good student, but I didn't see the profit in attending Hebrew school on any kind of regular basis. Every now and then, a note was sent home detailing my truancy, after which, I usually had to attend at least the next few sessions. I don't recall actually learning any Hebrew or feeling any great sense of awe when I was made to study Torah. I went to Hebrew school because I had to go—and only when I couldn't find a way to ditch it.

I did have a Bar Mitzvah, only it was unlike any ceremony I'd seen or have seen since. It was mostly my grandmother's doing, as I recall. She came into my bedroom one Saturday morning, woke me up, and dragged me down to the synagogue. She did it without warning or ceremony. She quite literally took me by the ear and led me to the temple, where I discovered that I was to be bar mitzvahed that morning. I had no idea how to read Hebrew, or even what the ritual entailed, but there I was, surrounded by all these grave-looking men, standing before the Torah. Truly, it was a most incongruous scene. My grandmother retreated to the balcony because, in an Orthodox synagogue, the women were kept apart from the men. As the ritual unfolded, the men chanted lines I was meant to repeat. I figured it out soon enough. They chanted a line, and I echoed it. They moved the pointer against the ancient markings of the Torah scroll, and I pretended to follow along. It was the most remarkable charade, and yet for twenty minutes, that was how it went. Finally, I got through all the prayers and the readings, someone pronounced me a bar mitzvah, and there were congratulations all around. I even received a pen and pencil set from an uncle married to my mother's sister, for whom this rite of passage clearly meant a great deal more than it meant to me.

I received another token to mark the occasion, this one from my father—a 1909 ten-dollar gold piece, which I carry in my pocket to this day. I can't tell you how many times I've reached for that coin, twirled it through my fingers, and thought back to how things were between my father and me, how things were in general back then, and how far I've come since. The interesting thing is, I never meant to carry that coin with me from that moment forward, but I kept it close, one day to the next, and before I knew it, those days had added up. Now, the gold piece is worth far more than its original ten dollars, and yet its value to me far exceeds any appraisal, for it draws a link between the boy I was and the man I've become, the man my father imagined.

Life, for the most part, was good. I was an extremely shy young man, withdrawn in most unfamiliar situations, and yet I managed to make and keep a few close friends. There was a roof over our heads. I even was able to go to college; I went to the University of Washington on a basketball scholarship, of all things. I suppose, in this one regard at least, I was lucky. I was a reasonably good athlete—nothing like I'd have to be today to earn a scholarship, but strong enough to hold my own in the basketball style of the late 1930s. The Depression was raging, and higher education was a luxury we could not have afforded on our own dime, but I had a high school friend who played football for the University of Washington. He mentioned to one of the coaches there that he had a friend back home who was a decent basketball player, and he was able to finagle a scholarship for me. I was never more than a decent ballplayer, but it was a different game. It was all about set shots and set plays. After every basket, we still took the ball back to center court for a jump ball. I was a smart guard and a solid defensive player. I usually was matched against the other team's top scorer, and I usually was able to contain him. That was my role, and I played it well enough. We weren't exactly a power-house team, but we held our own, and I managed to make a contribution.

In those days, of course, a scholarship applied only to tuition, so I had to scramble to meet my other expenses. I made a friend whose father kept a riverboat on Lake Washington, and we worked out a deal that allowed me to live on the boat in exchange for keeping an eye on it and keeping it clean. I scurried around, picking up odd jobs where I could—hauling, loading, cleaning—and, on top of that, my mother was able to send me twenty dollars each month to keep me afloat. Now, twenty dollars per month doesn't sound like too terribly much, but I was able to stretch it out, combine it with my other uncertain incomes, and live pretty nicely. That was until I got a call from home three weeks shy of gradua-tion telling me that my father had taken ill, my mother couldn't work because she needed to care for him, and I needed to come home straightaway. My father had a kidney problem that was very serious at the time. As it turned out, happily, he recovered from his illness and managed to return to another new line of work. But at just that moment, in the spring of 1940, it fell to me to keep the family going.

And so, I talked with my advisor, who suggested I skip out on the last weeks of school and return home to look for work.

It's always been a fascination to me to consider how we arrive at our life-altering crossroads, how we make the decisions that redi-rect the course of our days going forward. For me, I was standing at the corner of State and Madison in downtown Chicago, direct-ly in front of a Walgreens drug store. I was at a true crossroads

*Leonard H. Lavin,
shortly before the war*

in every sense, the intersection of hope and possibility. It was
April, or perhaps May, of 1940, and I was pounding the streets,
looking for a job, trying to figure a way to make a decent living
to help out my family and to launch some kind of career. To be
sure, there weren't a whole lot of prospects. The country was just
coming out of the Depression. War was on the horizon. As I considered my next move, I turned to face the Walgreens window,
and I started to think of the products I saw on display. I don't
know what had me thinking in just this way, but there it was. I
noticed all the lipsticks and nail polish and hair products. I
thought to myself, no matter what's going on in the rest of the
world—the Depression, the war in Europe—American women will
find a way to scrape some pennies together to buy these products
and make themselves look nice. It was a simple fact of our culture,
and the toiletries industry struck me, just then, as a recession-
proof niche, a sure bet in hard times.

This type of thinking was a bit of a departure for me. Understand, I had no formal training in marketing or sales. Plus, I

wasn't exactly the type to look at the world from any kind of big-picture perspective. I looked at what needed to be done, and I tried to go out and do it. But, for some reason, on this one score, I got to thinking how women's cosmetics might hold some sort of future for me, so, on an impulse, I hurried inside the drug store and made for one of the phone booths along the side wall. In 1940, all drug stores had phone booths—goodness, when was the last time you saw a phone booth?—and all phone booths had telephone books, so I thumbed furiously through the *Yellow Pages* until I reached the listing for "cosmetics and toiletries". I ran my finger down the list of companies and stopped when I came to a listing for Lucien Lelong. I'd never heard of Lucien Lelong, but I was drawn to the name because it matched my initials: L.L. for Leonard Lavin. It fairly popped out from the page, and I actually thought to myself, hmmm, maybe there's something to this. Next, I noticed the address: 55 East Washington, just around the corner from the drug store.

I wasn't much for believing in signs from above or fate, but there was no denying the kismet in this search. I immediately replaced the phone book and ran out to the street to the Lucien Lelong offices, where I somehow managed to talk my way into a job without an appointment, a resume, or anything of the sort. Lucien Lelong, I quickly learned, was a fairly well-known but still upstart fragrance house run by a fellow named Joe Stein. He was developing a line of fragrances he hoped to market under the name of this French couturier. It was a nascent operation all the way, and I signed on as the company's first office boy. I was also the first salesman and the first window trimmer. He had me do everything, before too long, and I meant to do it all well. My first salary was twelve dollars per week, which was a small fortune to me back then. It was enough, certainly, to keep up with the family expenses and to put away a little something for myself, besides.

Let me tell you, it was an education, learning the cosmetics business from such a ground-floor perspective. And, the more I worked at it, the more I confirmed my hunch on the corner of

*Leonard H. Lavin,*
*World War II, U.S. Navy*

State and Madison. Women just couldn't get enough of this stuff, no matter what the world picture looked like. Perfumes, lipsticks, nail polish—they were small-change items, to be sure, but they added up pretty quickly. Women wanted to look good, and any business catering to their desire to look good seemed to hold promise. Here again, I went back to my father's all-important lesson at Wrigley Field, which, by now, had grown to include a few more related truths: bet only on yourself, trust your hunches, play your best hand.

Unfortunately, these hunches had to be put on hold for the war in Europe. By the spring of 1941, I registered for the service, along with most everyone else my age. I drew a low draft number, so I knew that I would be called, and I was of two minds on this prospect. I didn't mind the thought of serving my country or fighting the good fight; in fact, I welcomed it, but I didn't want to have to slink through the mud for months on end. Blind patriotism only took me so far; I wanted to be able to take a shower each day. I thought if I allowed my tour of duty to be determined by the draft, I'd pull the kind of grunt work for which I didn't think I was particularly well suited. I found a friend who shared this view, and together we went down to the Navy recruiting office and enlisted. I'd never been any place to speak of, other than my hitch out in the state of Washington, and I allowed myself to think a bit how exciting the next years would be, seeing the world on the government's ticket. Remember, back in 1941, it was a great honor for a young man to fight for this country. That kind of pride and devotion to duty changed somewhat in the decades that followed, with our unpopular and uncertain efforts in the Korean and Vietnamese Wars, but we were all unabashedly patriotic when I was a young man. I was no different.

Ironically, I was first sent to the University of Chicago—so much for seeing the world—where I spent ninety days in training. After that, I was shipped to Norfolk for further assignment. From there, I was sent to a naval ship operating out of Guantanamo Bay, Cuba. There, I learned one of the first rules of the sea: when you're in the Navy, whether you're a passenger on a ship or a member of the crew, you have to work your way across. Literally. En route to Cuba, where I was due to join my ship at Guantanamo, I had to paint the side of the ship before I got there. They put me on a scaffold, strapped me into some ropes, handed me a bucket of paint, and lowered me down. There I was, hanging off the side of the ship, with one hand clutching the paintbrush and the other flailing wildly for balance. I think I got more paint on myself than I managed to brush onto the vessel.

At some midpoint of this ordeal, I heard the boatswain holler, "Hey, Lavin. Time for chow!"

It was a welcome call indeed. "Pull me up!" I shouted back.

"We don't pull anybody up," came the reply.

"What about lunch?" I wondered, no doubt futilely.

"Come and get it," I heard.

And so, I laid down my brush on the scaffolding and pulled myself up, fist over fist, careful not to bang against the wet paint on the side of the ship. It was tough going, let me tell you, with the way I was determined not to swing against the vessel, but I must have been hungry enough because I eventually made it.

I don't wish to dwell on my time in the service here because many writers much more talented than myself have committed to the printed page war stories far more exciting than the ones I have to tell. This is meant, after all, to be a book about my experiences in business, so I will offer merely a broad-strokes account. I was engaged, in all, in nine invasions. Each of these was dramatic, but some were naturally more dramatic than others. For example, we made an invasion in the South Pacific early in 1943, and we were on an attack transport. A group of marines came up to our ship ferrying three Japanese prisoners lying flat on their stomachs. The prisoners wore only loincloths and evidently had been captured after the bombardment. We all lined up on the railing and looked down as the three hardly dressed Japanese prisoners were brought aboard our ship. I was up on the signal bridge surveying the scene when, all of a sudden, one of the marines on our ship pulled out his weapon and—boom! boom! boom!—shot all three of the prisoners. Just like that. It turned out later, in the investigation that followed, that the fellow who did the shooting had lost a brother on the USS *Arizona*. He was emotionally distraught over his personal loss and the attack at Pearl Harbor, and he took it out on the Japanese in this way. As I recall, nothing happened to the marine as a result of his attack on the prisoners, but the moment stayed with me for the way it illustrated the up-close brutality and inhumanity we were all made to endure. It was a time of war, and it was just one incident among many, but my mind snapped a mental picture of that moment that it hasn't been able to shake for almost sixty years.

And here's another dramatic scene I'll never shake: I was on the attack transport USS *DuPage* shortly after the invasion of the

Philippines when we suddenly were called to our battle stations. It was the middle of the night, as pitch dark as could be, and we'd already been through a number of air raids without incident, but this one was different. I went up to my station on the bridge, where we had these twin 40 mm guns, and from the corner of my eye, I saw a dark object. I hit the deck, and as I went down, a kamikaze plane collided with the bridge. It was a devastating attack, costing us many, many lives, including some of my friends, and yet, by some miracle, I was spared. One of my closest friends was a pharmacist's mate on the ship. He came up from the medical quarters to see the fireworks, and as he stood on the fantail, a piece of shrapnel from the attacking plane flew off in his direction and beheaded the poor fellow. Just sliced his head right off. It was a horrifying thing. The plane also dropped a five-hundred–pound bomb on board, which somehow did not go off. A group of men managed to lift the thing and throw it over the side before it detonated.

The aftermath to this sad story is that, recently, my wife and I were on holiday deep sea fishing with some good friends, and we were sitting on the deck reading. I was reading a novel that happened to tell a similar story to what had occurred on that ship all those years ago, and, all of a sudden, I started to cry. I couldn't help myself. It was an eerily similar passage, and it just hit me, and I couldn't stop crying. I guess you become so hardened to what you see and experience during wartime that it takes the perspective of time and distance to soften you up to it.

After that kamikaze attack, the ship was on fire for a few days, and, during that time, the rest of the fleet left us for fear of follow-up attacks. I stayed with that ship for more than two years, and, for a good stretch of that time, we were being refitted in a two-bit Navy yard in the South Pacific. Finally, the ship returned to San Francisco, and I was able to go back to Chicago on leave.

Once there, I met a girl. Life moved quickly during the war, especially aspects of a romantic nature, and, all around me, friends and fellow enlisted men got caught up in whirlwind relationships. It seemed like the thing to do, to have a girl back home waiting to marry you after the war, so I allowed myself to get caught in the same swirl and proposed. Her name was Gloria, and I raced out and bought her an engagement ring. I no longer recall precisely what drove me to this determination, but I felt strongly that I should propose to this girl, double-time. I was due to head out to San Francisco, and I wanted to have this matter settled. It wasn't the most romantic proposal in the history of proposals, but it did the trick, and it took me out of circulation for the balance of my time in the service. Gloria was a good girl, and I was good and loyal to her. Besides, after we met, there were not a lot of port stops for rest and relaxation—not for me anyway.

Let me first close the book on my tour of duty before detailing how it was that this engagement didn't turn out to be the shrewdest move of my young life. There is one joyful, serendipitous moment I wish to include for the way it stands out against the brutality of those nine invasions. The moment took shape one lazy afternoon during the period of time I remained with our ship following that kamikaze attack. We were in the habit of filling our off-duty hours lazing about these wonderful spits of sand in the South Pacific, and on this particular day, I paddled out to one on a launch with my friend Jack Ehrlich, with nothing in mind but to relax and unwind. We brought along a couple of beers to pass the time, and as we lay there in the sun daydreaming and such, we got to thinking. Jack was a talented fellow, somewhat musically inclined, and as we lay on the beach, we started to invent song lyrics about home and friends and the beach where we were relaxing. Jack, who had been an orchestra leader before his time in the service, hummed out a simple melody, and the two of us came up with some passable lyrics.

I was about as musically inclined as a conch shell, but we were fairly caught up in the moment, and we felt we'd written a wonderful song. At least, we thought it was wonderful after our couple of beers, and, for the next few days, we hummed it, tinkered with the lyrics, and got it just right. We couldn't get it out of our heads, and the next time we were in San Francisco on leave, we wandered into the NBC radio station there to see about giving our song a proper hearing. We found a staff organist to accompany Jack on vocals. I couldn't carry a tune if it was cinched in a brown paper sack, so I sat it out. We made a recording of it, mostly as a novelty item. In those days, they made a metal record. I sent my platter home to Chicago for safekeeping and promptly forgot about it. Some time later, we got a letter on the ship from a song plugger offering to buy it for one thousand dollars, but we had no use for the money at sea, so we didn't answer and, frankly, forgot about it. And that would have been that if it hadn't been such a catchy number.

After I was out of the service and was making sales calls across the country, I heard the song on the radio. Someone recorded the song and had a big hit with it on the Warner Brothers label. I called Jack, who was then living on Long Island, and he had heard it too. We couldn't understand it. We were caught between being thrilled that something we'd cooked up as a lark on a lazy afternoon had made it to the radio and incensed that we'd been taken advantage of this way. I consulted a fellow I had met through a cousin shortly after I was married, Abe Lastfogel. At that time, he was the chairman of the William Morris agency, and I asked him to look into the matter. After we gave him a copy of our original recording, he managed to get to the bottom of things and came back to us with an offer of twenty-five thousand dollars, which represented a one-time payment for all rights to the song. Jack Ehrlich and I both felt that our shares wouldn't exactly amount to much or change our lifestyles going forward, and, on Abe's advice, we rejected the offer. We felt we had nothing to lose and a strong argument for better terms. After all, my mother still had a copy of that original metal recording back in Chicago, and it wouldn't do for Warner Brothers to be seen taking advantage of a pair of song-writing servicemen. Eventually, Abe negotiated a settlement for us of fifty thousand dollars, which we all felt was fair and a fairly significant payday for a few hours of work on a sun-drenched sandbar. In retrospect, the one-time "kill fee" didn't come close to what the song ultimately was worth. The song has been recorded dozens of times by some top-level entertainers, and if Jack and I had held out for some kind of royalty payments, we would have done well indeed.

As it was, though, fifty thousand dollars was nothing to be ashamed of. We had to renounce all rights to the song, drop all claims of authorship, and, in fact, promise that we would never allow either of our names to be associated with it. Since we weren't out to make careers in the song-writing game, this didn't trouble us in the least. Today, the song is now credited to another writing team entirely. I've kept my end of the deal, and I'll keep it now. But you'd recognize it if you heard it.

I still hear the song from time to time on oldies radio stations or piped into elevators or shopping centers. Whenever I do, I'm taken back to that lazy afternoon on that spit of sand, that point of pause in the great tumult of the war, and I'm always grateful for the memory.

The circumstances of my leaving the service were somewhat interesting, although I must admit that I am not proud of how my actions make me appear. I set them out here, though, to present the full picture of the young man I was so that I might measure it against the man I have become. After more than four years in the service, I was fairly itching to return to civilian life. The first atom bomb had been dropped, and I felt the war's end was near. I had done my time and my duty, and I was anxious to get started with the rest of my life. One day while on liberty, I was walking down Market Street in San Francisco past all the naval buildings, and I knew the war was winding down. I started to think I'd like to get out of my post as quickly as possible. Without really thinking things through, I turned into one of the buildings and inquired of the yeoman where I might find the communications officer. I followed the yeoman's directions past a series of desks and offices, and, once there, I asked to be directed to the communications officer of Western Sea Frontier.

They gave me the name of the rear admiral in charge, and I asked to see him. This was all out of the blue; I had no idea what I hoped to ask this gentleman once I received an audience with him. If you had asked me just then what the devil I was doing, I couldn't have told you.

"Tell him I bring regards from Captain McGrath in Guam," I said when asked what I wanted to see the rear admiral about. To this day, I don't know how I came up with it, but that is what happened. I just made it up. There wasn't even a Captain McGrath.

After a few moments, I was led past a series of offices to see the rear admiral. The man was gracious enough about my visit, but, after a bit, he asked me, "Chief, what is it that I can do for you?"

So I told him about my service, how I had been in Guam, how we had made the landing there, and how I'd made the acquaintance of this Captain McGrath. "We got to talking, sir," I said, "and the captain asked me if I ever got to San Francisco to please head up to Western Sea Frontier and offer his regards."

"Well, thank you," the rear admiral said. "And how is Captain McGrath?"

I allowed myself a small smile at this, realizing that my small sham had passed a big hurdle. I told the rear admiral that the captain was doing very well, and as I dug myself deeper into this hole, it occurred to me that I had done more than clear a hurdle—I was about to finish the race. At this point, I still had no idea what I'd hoped to get out of all this, but there was no turning back, so I kept it up. Finally, the rear admiral asked if there was anything he could do for me since I had gone to all this trouble to bring him regards from the fictitious captain.

I was all over the opportunity. I said, "Well, sir, I've been stationed on the *DuPage* for two years now, and as you know, our roster is filled, and there's no one who can get promoted until there's some movement off the ship. We have a very good crew, sir, and it's a shame that so many men are stalled at their present positions."

"Is there something else you would like to do?" he asked, quite reasonably.

Notice that I didn't ask for reassignment, but was merely responding to this man's opening. I offered that I would like to be an instructor in communications, and the rear admiral seemed to give this some consideration. He made sure to make a note of my name, and we made our good-byes.

The next day, I was back aboard our ship, and I heard my name over the loudspeaker. "Lavin," I heard, "come up to see the captain at once." I had no idea what this was about. I'd put the mischief of the day before out of my mind, and this call to my superior officer struck me as if from nowhere.

Well, this man was steamed. He had turned down transfers before. In fact, he was famous for turning down transfers. He had an experienced crew and didn't want to lose anyone off the ship. He had a piece of paper in his hand, and he shook it at me. "What the hell have you been doing?" he hollered.

"I don't know what you're talking about, sir," I stammered. This much, anyway, was true.

At this, he read my transfer order to Treasure Island, San Francisco, for further assignment to Bainbridge, Maryland. I shrugged my shoulders to indicate that this was indeed as much a surprise to me as it was to him, although, by now, I couldn't claim complete ignorance of the matter. The captain was absolutely enraged. He gave me a good chewing out, and, at the other end of it, he said, "Now, go down to your quarters, get your bag, and get off this goddamned ship in a half an hour or you'll never leave!"

To this day, I don't know what possessed me to go after my reassignment in just that way, but there it was—and it didn't turn out to be half bad. I was transferred to Treasure Island, then, about a week later, to Bainbridge, Maryland, where I was to be an instructor in communications. To me, it was like I'd died and gone to heaven. See, they used to have a racetrack out near the base there called Laurel Park, and I was out there most every day for a few weeks, playing the horses, learning to live like a civilian once more. Of course, this particular piece of the good life didn't last terribly long because soon after my arrival, we dropped the second atom bomb, and the war was essentially over. I got my papers a short time after that, and, for years after my discharge, I wondered if I had done something shameful, pulling that little charade with the rear admiral the way I did. As I stated at the outset, I'm not proud of this behavior, but it was who I was at the time and how I approached the world.

Good things don't necessarily come to those who wait, I determined, and I guess I was just tired of waiting.

Now, let me return to the matter of my engagement to this young woman. Here I'd frittered away all these opportunities by being faithful to Gloria only to return to find that her mother found me an unsuitable suitor. My position at Lucien Lelong was waiting for me, and the company had grown somewhat during the war. A lot of Mr. Stein's competitors had been unable to get supplies out of Europe, but he had been able to get essential oils out of Vichy, France, when it was under German control. He continued to supply stores with his product, so I came back to a viable, growing company. I was slated to be a salesman at something close to the salary I drew when I enlisted. In fact, before I resumed work, Mr. Stein asked me what I wanted to earn. I was young and cocky, so I thought I'd shoot for the moon. "Fifty dollars a week," I said, thinking this a small fortune. At this, Mr. Stein smiled, shook his head, and offered me seventy-five dollars per week, plus commissions. So much for shooting for the moon.

It was, I thought, a decent job with fairly decent prospects, but Gloria's mother thought otherwise. She took me aside one night when I came calling on her daughter and gave it to me straight. "Leonard," she said, "you're a nice boy, but I don't think you can keep my Gloria in the style to which she's become accustomed."

I thought, this woman has got to be kidding. True, I didn't have a pot to pee in, but few people did in those days. And it wasn't as though Gloria came from any kind of rich family. She lived modestly and didn't appear to focus on material possessions; she might have had a pot to pee in, but that was about it. Gloria's father was a movie house projectionist, for goodness sake! It was a good enough job, with a particularly strong union, but it was not the sort of job to place Gloria's mother on the kind of high horse she seemed to be riding. And yet I was in no position to argue. If Gloria wasn't going to fight on my behalf—and initial indications seemed to suggest she would not—I couldn't see the profit in talking my way into her family. I'll give Gloria credit, though; she was gracious enough to return the diamond engagement ring I gave her some months earlier, and that ring turned out to stake me in business.

Soon after my return to the fold at Lucien Lelong, I was asked to make a presentation on behalf of the company at the Ambassador Hotel in Chicago. I had to address a roomful of salespeople, who, in addition to our line of fragrances, also marketed other related products. My talk, which was intended to position our brand as a market leader in its price category, went over reasonably well. A number of people came up to me afterward to talk about the company, and among them was an elderly gentleman who waited patiently for the rest of the sales force to disperse. I remember him as elderly now, but, in truth, he must have been about fifty-five years old. Perspective, I suppose, is everything. In those days, when I was not yet thirty, fifty appeared positively ancient; today, I consider everything I didn't know at fifty and think of it as an age of youth and inexperience. In any event, this fellow put an arm around me, told me how impressed he'd been with my presentation, and mentioned he had an interesting new product he'd like to talk to me about at my convenience. I suggested that my convenience coincided neatly with just that moment, but the gentleman wanted to schedule a more formal meeting up in his office, so we made an appointment for the following afternoon. He did let on that he was onto a new type of permanent waving, and he wanted to demonstrate the technique for me himself. "This is really something you must see, Mr. Lavin," he insisted.

I thought, what the hell. I had nothing to lose. I had a promising arrangement with Lucien Lelong, but, frankly, I wasn't all that keen on working for someone else for the whole of my career. And I could see down the road far enough to know that I'd never be more than a salaried hand there; it was a place to start, but it was by no means where I wanted to end up. So, I went home, learned what I could about permanent waving, and waited for our appointment to tick around on the clock. Permanent waving was a great big deal just after the war, and the convention was for women to spend half a day or so at the beauty parlor in order to achieve just the right curl or "wave" in her hair. The key to a successful permanent was the intense application of heat for an extended period of time. There were a few companies starting to experiment with a so-called "cold" wave, which allowed the customer to achieve the same effect with a certain kind of chemical instead of heat in a fraction of the time.

I went up to this gentleman's office at the appointed time. His name was Frank Hall, and I found out later he was one of the original partners of the F.W. Woolworth company. He walked me through his new product, a home permanent wave kit, and I thought it was simply fantastic. The whole routine took an hour or so in the comfort of your own home. There was a special thermal heat pad built in to a series of rollers, and the idea was to allow the chemicals to set for a period of time, roll the hair with the special rollers, put a clip over it, and, in twelve minutes, you had a salon-quality curl. It doesn't sound like much now, but back then it was a tremendous innovation. I've come to pride myself on my ability to recognize unique items or applications and bring them to market. This was really my first opportunity to do so.

"You've really got something here," I said to Mr. Hall, not wanting to let on the lengths of my enthusiasm.

"That's what I thought you'd say," he replied.

"No, really," I insisted, as if my two cents amounted to much of anything. "It could revolutionize the industry."

At this, Frank Hall simply nodded, which I took to mean I had no business telling him what he already knew.

"And why is it you wanted me to see this new product?" I asked, redirecting the conversation back to where I had some place in it.

"Well, Leonard," he said, "I was hoping you'd like to come to work for me." He didn't put this in the form of a question, he just set it out for me to consider. The moment he did, I realized I was tired of what I was doing with Lucien Lelong. Tired of the routine. Tired of the prospects. Just plain tired. I ran all kinds of numbers in my head and grew quietly excited at the idea of signing on with Frank Hall and his home permanent kits.

"Just what did you have in mind?" I wondered.

What he wanted, he said, was someone to help him achieve nationwide distribution. He had a whole marketing plan in place, and all he needed was an aggressive, visionary young salesman to carry it out. His idea was to open a key account in every American city with a population more than fifteen thousand. For every account opened, he would pay a one-time fee of fifty dollars. On top of that, he was offering one hundred dollars per week for expenses.

Well, that sounded just fine with me, so we shook hands right then and made a deal. All that was left was for me to get a car, and that's where Gloria's engagement ring came in. I traded it in for an old Studebaker. The inside of the car smelled like a French whorehouse. I'd never been to a French whorehouse, so I suppose it would be more accurate to suggest it smelled how I *thought* a French whorehouse might smell. The dealer told me the Studebaker was owned by a school teacher during the war, so I took him at his word and bought the car. I needed some way to get from city to city, and if it meant traveling in a car of dubious origin, who was I to quibble if the price was right?

And besides, as I made ready to leave the fragrance business for the home perm game, the irony of criss-crossing the country in a car that smelled of cheap perfume was not lost on me.

***

I never meant to become a traveling salesman, but that was pretty much the size of my new position with Frank Hall, and I determined not to make a cliché out of it. I had my years of Navy discipline from which to draw, and they steeled me with a resolve and purpose I would not have had otherwise. See, up until my time in the service, I was what used to be called a wild kid. I never got into any real trouble or anything like that, but I was given to flights of fancy and was somewhat disorderly in my approach to adult, professional situations. I was the sort of kid who might put off until tomorrow what he might otherwise accomplish today. After the war, though, I saw the world a little differently, and my role within it also was changed. I meant to make a difference, to leave my mark. To build something that would outlast my time on this Earth. And I meant to do it soon.

The name of the product I was selling was Beauty Wave, and it came packaged in a kit that consisted of curlers, pads, and a bottle of lotion. It sold for $3.95 retail, and it was good for one home permanent wave treatment—a fraction of the cost of a salon perm, with do-it-yourself convenience. I also peddled refill units, which carried only the pads and the lotion; these sold for $1.00 retail and allowed the customer to achieve a second home perm with the original curlers. Beyond that, the customer had to go out and purchase another kit for a subsequent use because the curlers were made with pieces of cloth and could not easily withstand a third treatment.

I tallied my first expense vouchers with the purchase of a series of fine road maps and a book put out by the Department of Commerce. The book carried the names, addresses, and telephone numbers of leading retail, drug, and department stores in every municipality. (I believe these books are still published, up-dated annually.) The book paid for itself my first day on the road. It listed the size of each store, what kind of merchandise it sold, and in what volume. It really was an indispensable tool, and before I finished covering the country a year and a half later, the thing was so dog-eared and out of date I had to buy another.

I attempted to move from town to town in a systematic way, only this wasn't always so easy. There were an awful lot of towns with populations approaching fifteen thousand in those days. The big cities were no-brainers—New York, Philadelphia, Baltimore, and so on—but there were tougher sales to be made in the country's midsection, in more rural areas. What I found, for the most part, was that buyers in larger metropolitan areas were more so-phisticated in their tastes and more willing to take a chance on a new product. Small-town merchants tended to give their cus-tomers what they'd always wanted, rather than what they might want instead. Nevertheless, I never missed a sale. Mind you, I was turned down from time to time, but if a buyer rejected my initial pitch, I asked to see the vice president of merchandising, or what-ever the appropriate title was at a given store. If he turned me down, I made an appointment with the president or the owner of the store. I refused to take no for an answer, and here again, this was my Navy discipline at work. I had my eye on a clear and stat-ed goal, and I never missed once. I never even had to cross the street to sell my wares to a lesser competitor. I told myself I had to make that fifty-dollar fee, and it had to be with the biggest, most prominent store in town. And I did.

Before I set out for the open road, Frank Hall outfitted me with an ample supply of hair samples, which had been carefully glued together in small bunches. He told me it was "virgin" hair purchased from a convent of nuns outside Chicago, and I believed him. Why wouldn't I believe him? Anyway, it made a nice pres-entation, and the whole virgin hair aspect became an important part of my spiel. In some rare instances, a buyer placed an order without a formal presentation, but, for the most part, it fell to me to put this virgin hair to use. I'd breeze into town, target a store, ask to see the buyer, and set up my materials to demonstrate how easy it was to achieve a home permanent. I'd make a grand showing of timing the whole thing. I'd take out a strand of hair, treat it with lotion, curl it up, put a clip on it, and ask the buyer to look at his watch and tick off twelve minutes. I used this time to talk up some of the other benefits of the product and to go over pricing and some testimonials I'd collected along the way. When our time was up, I combed out the hair and encouraged the buyer to join me in marveling at the curl. I don't mean to sound flip about it because it truly was a revolutionary product, so much so that it almost sold itself.

The minimum order required to open an account was six dozen kits and three dozen refills, and I think one of the reasons I was so successful was that I seldom tried to overshoot my goal. The thinking was simply to get our product in the door and on the shelves, then let word-of-mouth carry us to the next reorder. I didn't have the time to waste to talk these buyers into placing bigger initial orders. They opened an account, I sent in the paperwork, and I was on my way to the next town. Some days, I was able to hit three or four cities, which amounted to a fairly significant take for a young fellow like myself. Two hundred dollars for a hard day's work was just about a small fortune, but, most days, I was limited by geography to one or two sales. And, of course, there were some days devoted entirely to travel. Wherever possible, I endeavored to make it to the next town by nightfall, so I could find a place to stay and awaken refreshed the next morning to greet the buyer when the store opened at nine o'clock. In those days, of course, department stores weren't open on Sundays, so I had one day a week to rest and refuel, although I didn't do much resting. I usually tried to work my itinerary so that my long travel days fell on a Sunday, so that I wouldn't miss making an early call.

I also determined never to spend a night in my Studebaker. Remember, this was the same guy who enlisted in the Navy for the chance it offered at a hot shower each day, so I wasn't exactly the roughing-it type. Hotel rooms were hard to come by back then, as was fuel in some out-of-the-way places, but I usually was able to find a decent motel, or, in some towns, a bed-and-breakfast type lodging. In particularly remote areas, like Brownsville, Texas, I wound up at a farmhouse or somesuch, although I can report here that I never slept with one of the farmer's daughters. There were some grand adventures, to be sure, during seventy-five weeks of this kind of living, but none so grand that they ended in a punch line, with a farmer pointing his rifle at my sorry hide and chasing me from his property.

I attempted to live a fairly Spartan existence to stretch my hundred dollar weekly stipend as far as it would go, and in this I was mostly successful. The money was just about enough to cover gas and lodging, and where it failed to make ends meet completely was over meals. I told myself I had to eat anyway, at home or on the road, and deemed this an acceptable shortfall, but I sought out inexpensive luncheonettes and diners just the same. Sometimes, when money was especially tight, I made do with one or two meals a day, instead of the usual three square.

When I returned to Chicago, after about a year and a half of this vagabonding existence, I still hadn't collected a penny other than my regular expense checks. I'd accumulated a lot of money on the books—approximately fifty thousand dollars, representing about one thousand accounts—but I hadn't seen any of it just yet. When income tax time rolled around, I listed all those expense payments as income. I mention this to demonstrate that even a soon-to-be-successful businessman can make a stupid mistake, but so be it. And the thing with me is I always learned from my mistakes, so you can be sure I never made this one again.

Frank Hall was good to his word, however, and over the moon with excitement at how I covered the country for him. He was only too happy to pay me the fifty thousand dollars he owed me. I think my traveling sales show exceeded his wildest expectations, and the first thing he did when I got back to his office was offer me a full-time job with the company. The understanding, with these accounts, was that I wouldn't participate in any reordering or continuing business. As national sales manager, I'd be entitled to some sort of bonus compensation as our business grew. He offered me one hundred dollars a week to start, and I wasn't exactly bowled over by the proposal. See, I'd just earned more than six times that amount on the road, and I'd enjoyed those weeks immensely. Plus, I'd made so many contacts, it got me to thinking that the thing to do was introduce another innovative product to some of these same buyers on another whirlwind tour. I was still young. I wasn't married. There was nothing keeping me tied to Chicago beyond my roots.

"Mr. Hall," I responded, "I appreciate the offer, but if you don't mind, I'd like to think about it."

He was a smart man, Frank Hall, and an incredibly decent one as well. For some reason, he didn't want me to leave the fold. He wasn't out to cheat me with his salaried offer—after all, a fifty-two hundred dollar salary in 1947 was considered a very generous package—but he hadn't anticipated that I would take to the road as well as I had. For most, it was a kind of trial; for me, he could see, it had been a challenge and a thrill. So he upped the ante a bit. "I understand your hesitation, Leonard," he said, "so how about this? How about you come to work for me as my sales manager, and when you grow the company to two million dollars in sales, I'll give you 20 percent of the business."

Now, here was something a young fellow could get his mind around. Twenty percent of the business! Certainly, this was an exciting offer and an intriguing one as well. It awakened in me a desire I hadn't thought to articulate, or fully appreciate, until just that moment. I realized that what I truly wanted in this world was to go it alone. I wasn't cut out to be a salaried hand going through the same motions as everyone else. I wanted to out-think, out-hustle, out-sell the other guy and build a business that would out-pace my best-case scenarios. There was an entrepreneur somewhere inside of me, bursting to get out, and it took all those months on the road to figure it out. My father's backhanded ballpark counsel echoed once more: don't let others call the shots for you; bet on yourself; go it alone.

At this point in my young career, I didn't have the resources to go out on my own completely—not just yet—but I looked on this Beauty Wave opportunity as the next best thing. "Mr. Hall," I said, extending my hand to seal the deal, "you've got yourself a new sales manager."

By my calculations, I figured we'd reach that two million dollar sales threshold in no time flat.

# 2

---

# Getting Started

I ALWAYS WILL BE GRATEFUL TO GLORIA'S MOTHER FOR REJECTING ME and my career prospects because if it hadn't been for her, I never would have met and married my beautiful wife Bernice. And if it hadn't been for Bernice, I never would have built my business to its present prominence. Everything's connected, don't you think? One door closes and another one opens—in life, and in business. And as often as not, it works out for the best.

I met Bernice at a dance in the summer of 1947, and I was drawn to her immediately. Have you ever met someone for the first time and felt immediately comfortable with that person? Like you've known each other your entire lives? Or, here's a better way to put it: like you were *meant* to know each other your entire lives? Well, that's how it was with Bernice and me. She was a beautiful young woman and way out in front in terms of her career. She worked for a fellow named Arnold Maremont, who was a big Chicago industrialist. He had a company called Maremont Automotive, which made springs, mufflers, transmissions, and other car parts for General Motors, Chrysler, Ford, and all the big automobile companies at the time. When I met Bernice, she was the comptroller of the entire operation, which was a fairly big job for such a young girl. She was only twenty years old, but she was a tremendous asset to the company. She had been working in the accounting department, and her boss, the comptroller, told her

*Bernice Lavin,
1960s*

he was going to take the exam to become a certified public accountant. Sure enough, he failed the exam. He took it a second time and failed again. For the third attempt, he suggested to Bernice that she help him study and take the exam with him. Wouldn't you know it, the poor guy failed again, and Bernice passed with flying colors. (That's my girl!) So Bernice became the comptroller, which worked out well for her, even if it wasn't exactly what her boss had in mind.

I should mention here that Bernice was equally happy that Gloria's mother cut me loose—and never more so than some years later, long after we were married and long after my company, Alberto-Culver, became an established company. I was in the hospital for an extended period, recovering from internal bleeding and undergoing some related tests, and my private room was over-flowing with flowers, candy, and cards. I was a somewhat promi-nent Chicago citizen by then, and news of my hospitalization spread to my many friends and business associates. At one point, one of the other patients wanted to know who it was on the re-ceiving end of all those well wishes. When she learned that the president of the Alberto-Culver Company was on the unit, she was determined to meet me. She used our products at home, and so she made it a point to drop in and say hello. Well, it turned out that this inquisitive patient was Gloria's mother, from all those years ago. She did not remember me by name, but I quickly re-minded her who I was and how she had sent me packing. Well, her mouth opened in astonishment, and if she had had false teeth they would have dropped to the floor. The poor woman turned red, and then she turned tail. I don't mean to toot my own horn, but I was reasonably certain I was finally earning enough money to have kept her Gloria comfortable—and the way my reputation had apparently preceded me, the woman who had rejected me as a son-in-law concurred with this assessment.

When Bernice came by to see me later, I told her of the en-counter, thinking she'd find it amusing as well. Instead, she was a little bit incensed that someone had pushed aside her husband for no good reason, even if it was all ancient history and had turned out for the best. The next day, still fuming, Bernice came to the hospital dressed to the nines, wearing every piece of ex-pensive jewelry I gave her during our time together: rings on all fingers, necklaces, pins, earrings. She had on every imaginable thing, which was totally out of character for her. She wore an enormous amount of jewelry, topped by a gorgeous fur coat of some kind, and she paraded onto the unit and asked to see the patient by name. Then, she walked into the woman's room and introduced herself.

"I am Mrs. Lavin," she said, holding out her hands as if for a manicure, showing off all of her rings. "It's such a pleasure fi-nally to meet you." She fairly oozed a sense of satisfaction at this woman, and when I heard about it later, I secretly applauded Bernice for her lack of subtlety. *That* was the woman I fell for—all spunk and brass.

When I met Bernice, she was in a great circumstance, great shape, and great spirits, but she didn't have the easiest go of things as a child. Her parents were separated when she was young, which in those days was a very unusual situation, and it couldn't have been easy for her, growing up in a broken home. Moreover, she collapsed while going down a flight of stairs at nine or ten years old, which left her on her back for about two years. The fall was caused by a chronic condition known as septic arthritis, which severely limited her activity as a young girl. The Shriners financed a trip to Boston hospitals for her, where she got wonderful care, but was still away from home for an extended period. She suffered enormously as a child. My heart ached when she first told me the story of her childhood, but I think her various ordeals left her with a resolve and purpose she might not otherwise have had. She came through it stronger, if that makes any sense, and it was that strong, accomplished, forthright woman I fell in love with that summer.

For reasons I have not yet been able to determine, Bernice fell in love with me as well. We started dating and fell into an unusual routine. Most of my friends met their girlfriends for dinner after work, typically at a reasonable hour, but Bernice often worked until seven or eight o'clock in the evening, so we got together for late suppers. My friends all thought I was nuts to putter around all evening until Bernice was free for the night, but I simply told them they were the crazy ones for settling down with such conventional women. A working woman was doubly exciting. We moved about on common ground. We understood each other and each other's business. We really were a good match, and there was never any question in my mind that the thing to do was wait her out each evening. Plus, it gave me a few extra hours each day to catch up on paperwork or on my reading. Sometimes, I met Bernice up at her office with a picnic dinner, but usually we met at her home. We took long walks through the city, and, as we walked and talked, our conversation invariably turned toward the future. At one point, about three months into our relationship, I proposed the idea of marriage. I hadn't meant to, but it struck me as a reasonable plan. See, I was about to leave for Los Angeles on business, and I suggested that if we could somehow obtain a license and get married in the next day or so we could turn the trip into a honeymoon.

As soon as I said it, I knew this was pie-in-the-sky stuff. A part of me, I suppose, was only kidding around. I felt sure we would marry someday, and soon, but I knew we would do well to wait. We'd only been together a short while. When we talked around the subject, marriage was always well off into the future. Bernice had her career to think about, and I had mine. And besides, in those days, in Chicago as elsewhere, you needed a blood test to apply for a marriage license, and there was a minimum three-day waiting period before the city would grant a license. My impromptu, half-hearted proposal came on a Monday night, and I was due to leave on that Thursday. So, in my impish way, I suppose that I hoped to score points with Bernice by proposing and buy time—at least until I came back from my trip.

At least, that's how I assessed the situation, but Bernice saw things differently. She might have known I was half serious and partly playing, and she might have been half serious and partly playing herself, but she jumped at the idea. Before I knew what had happened, we were both caught up in it. Soon enough, we were talking through the logistics of the plan and we were fully serious and not playing at all. It felt to us, all of a sudden, like the right move, the *next* move—only we'd left ourselves no time at all to pull it off. At least, that's how it seemed to me when we parted company that night. Oh, we'd be married, sooner rather than later, but there were too many details to arrange before my trip that Thursday, just three days away. The wedding would have to wait on my return. There was simply too much red tape and not enough time to cut through it. Even if we could find a way to get around the city's three-day waiting period and get a marriage license, there'd be no way to land Bernice a seat on a flight out to California.

But I hadn't counted on Bernice. Goodness, if there was ever a woman who could turn an unlikely possibility into a certainty, it was my Bernice. Unbeknownst to me, she arrived at her desk that Tuesday morning and pulled whatever strings she could find, trying to get us around the various hurdles. She called her boss, Arnold Maremont, and had him reach out to the mayor, who cited special circumstances in waiving the three-day waiting period for a marriage license. Next, she asked Mr. Maremont to telephone a friend of his at TWA, who arranged it so that the poor fellow seated next to me on the Thursday flight was bumped to another flight. Then she called me at my office and announced, "We're getting married on Thursday."

I must admit, she caught me completely by surprise—and happily so. I may have been kidding about making such hasty plans, but I learned that you don't joke about such a thing with a woman like Bernice. "How is that possible?" I asked.

She filled me in on the particulars. She even told me how she arranged for a ceremony and reception at the Drake Hotel, which was normally booked well in advance. As she did, I quietly congratulated myself for thinking to fall for such a high-powered, well-connected woman.

And so we were married that Thursday, October 30, 1947, to be precise (how's that for a late birthday present?), in a lovely ceremony in the Drake's Camellia Room. Bernice's mother managed to arrange a marvelous brunch on impossibly short notice. As Bernice and I exchanged vows, I thought to myself, well there you go, Lavin, kidding your way into a marriage with a woman you barely know. But, truly, I couldn't have been happier. Bernice may have turned the tables on me and made me put my money where my mouth was, but I was glad she did. And so, I felt certain, was she.

The whole thing happened so fast there was barely enough time to tell everyone the news. In fact, we didn't tell *everyone*. We didn't move in together right away. Some of our good friends were in the dark for quite some time. Even my boss, Frank Hall, didn't know we'd gotten hitched, and it nearly came back to bite us in the weeks ahead, as I will soon explain. For now, though, let me state for the record that our last-minute honeymoon was a good and remarkable thing, just as our marriage has been a good and remarkable thing. And, also for the record, let me tell the not-so-sordid details of our wedding night, making me, perhaps, the first head of a Fortune 500 company to kiss and tell such intimate details in book form: I gave Bernice a permanent. She was always somewhat intrigued by the Beauty Wave product and curious about how it worked, so on the first night of our marriage, I gave her a permanent wave. (How's that for romance?) The opportunity never came up before, and there was no better way to explain the process than to demonstrate it. I applied the lotion, rolled Bernice's hair up in curlers, and timed the whole thing out, just like I was making one of my presentations with the nuns' virgin hair. After twelve minutes, my young bride looked absolutely sensational, like one of those knockout "after" photos in a "before and after" advertisement—only in Bernice's case, the "before" shot wouldn't have been half bad, either.

As long as I was on the West Coast, I figured I'd mix in some business with our pleasure. So the next morning, I raced off to San Francisco on a sales call, while I left the new Mrs. Lavin behind in our Los Angeles hotel with her new perm to receive the extra attentions of the hotel staff. As soon as the people at the hotel found out she was a new bride who'd been left behind by her heartless, hard-working husband, they treated her like royalty—and Bernice didn't mind it much at all.

Back in Chicago, I worked diligently to beef up the sales of the Beauty Wave line. It was our one and only product, and we couldn't reach that two million dollar sales threshold quickly enough. I was on the road an awful lot during my courtship with Bernice and in the early days of our marriage, but that suited us both just fine. After all, she was a career woman; she understood the demands of the workplace and, in my case, the call of the road.

The routine was for me to lunch with Mr. Hall whenever we were both in town, and, on one of those afternoons, he took me down to his bank. We had lunch first at the Sheraton Hotel, a particular favorite of his, and, afterward, we went to the Wrigley Building Bank, where he kept a vault.

"There's something I want to show you, Leonard," he said.

I couldn't imagine what he had in mind. There was something clandestine about the whole thing. He took me back to his vault, where a teller handed him his locked box, and we walked with it to a private room. He set the box down on a table and pulled up a chair.

"Leonard," he said, opening the box, "I wanted to show you something I learned during the Depression." As he spoke, I saw inside the box, where he kept thousands of brand new one-hundred-dollar bills, neatly stacked. There were two million dollars, in all. I didn't count it, but took Mr. Hall at his word. "Cash is always important," he told me. "It's the one sure thing. Get yourself a foundation, and grow your efforts from there. You've got to speculate to accumulate, but you must always keep your foundation. Add to it when you can, or when you feel the need, but always keep your foundation money."

I'd never seen so much money all in one place. It was truly the most astonishing sight, and I started to think that some day it would be me heading down to my own vault to check on my own stores. Perhaps I'd have my own young protégé in tow and pass off some sage advice of my own. I'd yet to invest the fifty thousand dollars I earned by opening up all those markets for Beauty Wave, and I vowed right then to make that money my stake, my foundation, for whatever it was that would come next. I'd live on my salary and my expense account, and sock away what I could for my next move. I couldn't imagine how long it would take to increase this foundation to two million dollars as Mr. Hall apparently had done, but I fully expected to do so, and soon. It's funny how our perspectives change as we move forward in our goals. A couple of years earlier, I'd have stared wide-eyed at a stack of bills amounting to my own fifty thousand dollars, and here it all seemed to be within reach. It's strange, isn't it, the way the unthinkable begins to appear possible? That's the thing about far-off goals; you rise to meet them, one step at a time.

Meanwhile, the Beauty Wave line enjoyed solid growth in the marketplace. There were competing lines out there, but ours was the clear market leader. I felt confident that we soon would achieve our goal of two million dollars in sales. To that end, I worked tirelessly and traveled endlessly, and Bernice—great, good sport that she was—fully realized that this was the price she had to pay for marrying a salesman. Frank Hall, too, was a dedicated worker, and at some point in the middle of our constant back-and-forth-ing, I realized that Bernice and I had yet to tell him we'd gotten married. That was how our hasty marriage nearly came back to bite us, as I promised to tell earlier; I hated the thought of being found out, of having to look foolish or deceitful to a man who was so generous with his opportunities.

One warm Saturday afternoon, Bernice came up to meet me with a picnic basket. We were planning to take a walk on the beach and enjoy a nice lunch. While Bernice waited for me to finish up some paperwork, Mr. Hall crossed to my desk to make some small talk. It was unusual for the two of us to be in the office at the same time, and he apparently was feeling gregarious.

"Why don't you two kids get married?" he finally said, whereupon Bernice and I flashed each other a flustered look. Neither of us could think what to say, and so we said nothing, but Mr. Hall kept on with his notion. He liked Bernice, and he liked me, and he was just being kind. He had it in his head that he would see us married, and he kept on and on about it. He even offered to treat us to our honeymoon. He was a good, big-hearted man, and I hated like hell that we had deceived him for all these weeks. Of course, there were a lot of people we still hadn't told, and, as I recall, we were still looking for a place to live. My relationship with my boss wasn't exactly on a social basis, but I still felt badly about it. "You'll be off on business for me, Leonard," he continued, "and Bernice can come along. My treat."

Now, I had my standards, and I was raised to be a fairly ethical fellow, but I wasn't fool enough to turn down a second honeymoon, on the house. "Sounds good to me," I said. "How about you, Bernice?"

Bernice saw right away what I was up to and smiled sheepishly, as a girl might do when being proposed to for the *first* time, and we went through the whole rigmarole all over again. We didn't invite any guests this time around, but my parents were there. We had another full-blown ceremony, and we were sure to take pictures, so that we would have them to show Mr. Hall upon our return. As we went through these redundant motions, we considered that we were merely adding emphasis to an already emphatic point. We called it our "do-over" wedding, and we felt doubly blessed.

For our second honeymoon, we went out to San Francisco, and I took Bernice out to the fairgrounds for a day at the racetrack. She'd never been to the horse races before, and she found it fairly fascinating, so I was pleased to be able to share it with her. I told her everything she needed to know about the horses, and the jockeys, and the betting line, and she was a quick study. Right away, she was bitten by the same bug that had claimed me as a small boy; she wanted in on the action. She grabbed a racing program and picked out a horse: Loving Joy. She liked the name, she said. It spoke to her or reminded her of us or something. Of course, such reasoning as this wouldn't do for a seasoned player like myself, so I took the form and looked at the particulars. By this time, of course, I was an expert on horse racing, and I carried myself as such. Nobody could tell me a thing about handicapping, or so I thought. Loving Joy didn't have a chance in this field, I quickly noted, but I was careful not to say anything to Bernice. I didn't want to quiet her enthusiasm for the sport by telling her right out of the gate that she had no idea what she was doing.

"I want to bet two dollars across," she announced.

I'd explained to her that to bet a horse "across" meant to bet on the horse to win, place, *and* show. Three bets in all. If it came in a winner, you cashed in on your win bet, your place bet, and your show bet; if the horse fell slightly short and ran second or third, you were still in the money. Two dollars across meant a six-dollar wager, and I couldn't see handing over such a sum to race-track officials on such a miserable beast as Loving Joy, so I offered to book the bet for my young bride. To "book" a bet, in gambling parlance, meant to cover the wager. I wouldn't place the bet at the window, but I'd make good on it myself. If it lost, we wouldn't be out the six dollars. If it came in, I'd make good on the winnings.

Bernice said this would be fine with her—a bet was a bet—and we sat there enjoying the pleasant afternoon, waiting for the race to go off. Sure enough, it became a story that survived more than fifty years of retelling. Loving Joy came in first, and, like a mope, I didn't have the money to cover the bet. Bernice's total winnings came in at around seventy-five dollars, and I didn't walk around with that kind of money in those days.

Bernice—bless her!—was completely enthralled at her good fortune. "Pay up!" she demanded, with tremendous good cheer. I had to confess that my pockets were mostly empty and that she would have to extend me some credit, which she reluctantly did. Over the years, I paid off that bet many times, as if Bernice broke the bank, and I kick myself each time for talking her out of placing her bet at the windows as she intended. But it made a good story, from the first telling to this one, and as Loving Joy hurtled past the finish line ahead of the field, I actually thought back to Mr. Hall's foundation account at the vault in the Wrigley Building. I thought, this woman, my wife . . . she is my true foundation. My loving joy. I might have had fifty thousand dollars to my name (less seventy-five, of course), but, truly, I was so much richer than that. Truly, I was blessed with a stunning, steadfast, whip-smart woman who could discern an also-ran from a champion.

Whether I was thinking of myself or the surprising horse, I could not be entirely sure, but the foundation was set either way.

About a year into my full-time position with Frank Hall, the Beauty Wave line really took off. We did one million dollars in retail sales through the Montgomery Ward catalog alone, and I continued to service the accounts I set up during my initial tour of the country. To these, I added new accounts from time to time when we felt a need to bolster our distribution or to reach deeper into an under-performing marketplace. We were able to offer co-op advertising to our larger accounts, which meant that we supplied national copy and artwork to which the local merchant could add particular store information for hometown newspapers; in some cases, we also underwrote the cost of advertising placement.

All along, in the back of my mind, I held the thought of what it would mean when my 20 percent partnership kicked in as Mr. Hall had promised. When we neared our goal of two million dollars in sales, I watched our ledgers carefully, anxious for the day I could claim my share. Finally, that day arrived. It was late fall, and I returned to the city in triumph. I made sure Mr. Hall was in his office when I got there, and as I burst through the door, I extended my hand. "Hello, partner," I said.

It was a line I'd rehearsed for the last hundred or so miles of my return trip. I thought it would make a good impression and get our partnership conversation off on a positive note, but Mr. Hall looked at me blankly. "What are you talking about, Leonard?" he asked.

Of all the ways our conversation could have gone, this was not one I could have foreseen. Mr. Hall was pleasant enough, but he seemed to be operating on a different wavelength. I reminded him of our agreement and pointed out to him that we had crossed the two-million-dollar mark in sales. "I've been working very hard for you, Mr. Hall," I told him, "and I'm ready."

Indeed I was. It was Frank Hall who wasn't quite ready. To be fair and a bit more accurate, it wasn't as if he planned to welsh on our deal, he simply had a change in plans. He remembered his promise to me—he said so straight off—but something came up in the interim. "Sit down, Leonard," he said gently, and when I did, he told me how he and Mrs. Hall were thinking of retirement. He had bought some land in Beverly Hills, California, and they planned to build a home there. He knew he had an obligation to me, and he meant to honor that obligation in what ways he could, but surely I could understand how he couldn't keep working the business forever. "I'll tell you what," he said. "Instead of making you a 20 percent partner, how about I let you run the entire business instead?"

This sounded promising. "What would that mean?" I wondered.

"Well," he suggested, "I will pay you five hundred dollars a week and all expenses. You can take Bernice wherever you want, really live it up if you'd like. Take her to New York. Take her to California. The business will pay for it."

"What about equity?" I asked. This, to me, was key.

He told me he wasn't looking to grow the company beyond its present scope. He wasn't planning to add a new line or reach into new markets. "Just keep things the way they are, Leonard," he said, "and we'll be fine. I'm too old to want to build the business. Just keep it level."

Well, he might as well have told me he was fixing to close up shop. To an aggressive, market-building guy like myself, the status quo was anathema. You were nothing in business, I thought, unless you meant to be bigger, faster, harder, stronger. This, I suppose, was my Depression-era upbringing talking, or perhaps my Navy discipline; it's possible, too, it was a perspective gained during those long months on the road, opening up those thousand or so markets for Beauty Wave. I couldn't understand that type of thinking in business. I loved the idea of making a product grow. It was one thing to be content in your personal life, to have found the perfect partner and the perfect spot where together you could be content to live out your years; but in business, to my young thinking, there was never a good reason to rest on your laurels. What was the point of going to work if you weren't looking to build on your accomplishments from the day before? Frankly, it wasn't the comedown from a 20 percent stake in a two-million-dollar company to a five-hundred-dollar weekly salary that had me so disappointed; it was the absence of *opportunity* in the offer. The money was actually fine. In 1948–49, a twenty-six-thousand-dollar salary was nothing to sneeze at—and yet Mr. Hall's offer held absolutely no appeal.

I left his office a dispirited man, but I promised him I would think about it. I wasn't just thinking for myself, at this point. I had to consider Bernice's wishes on this latest turn. She was pregnant with our first child, and it was not unreasonable to assume she'd welcome the security of a steady paycheck over a roll of the dice. Plus, I wanted to talk the matter over with my parents, with whom I was still fairly close. For all his stops and starts in business, I valued my father's judgment. I had my own opinion, of course, but I welcomed his take on the matter as well.

Bernice understood my disappointment. It was hers as well. She encouraged me to do what I wanted, whatever would make me happy. I wasn't surprised by her support, but I was nevertheless grateful, so I took a practical view. We still had her salary from Maremont, which, at that time, was about two hundred fifty dollars a week, so there was a bit of a cushion if I wanted to go off and try something new. There was also my foundation money, the fifty-thousand-dollar stake I'd only recently vowed not to touch, but it loomed in the back of my thinking as a kind of safety net.

My parents thought I was completely nuts to consider walking away from a deal such as this. Five hundred dollars a week! For a no-pressure situation with a boss who had no expectations beyond keeping his operation running. With a baby on the way! It was, to them, the quintessential cushy job, offered at a time when the security was meaningful. They couldn't understand why it held no appeal.

But I looked on the Beauty Wave offer as selling out, and, at twenty-nine years old, I was too young to sell out. Maybe if I'd been older and more settled I would have felt differently. Maybe if I'd been a father, instead of just a father-to-be, I'd have grabbed at the security of the deal.

I wrestled with the dilemma for two days, after which I went in to see Mr. Hall and told him I could not accept his offer. I gave notice. I would leave the company at the end of the year, as a courtesy to him, and in that time—just about a month or so, as I recall—I would lay the groundwork for my next move. I had a plan in mind. I would start my own national sales company, the Leonard H. Lavin Sales Company. This was a relatively new concept at the time. In fact, I don't think there was another national sales company in the industry—at least not in the midwestern region. But, to me, it appeared to be a natural next move. I knew everybody across the country. I knew the head of every drug chain, the head of every department store. I knew all the buyers.

All I needed was to go out and get some products to represent on a national basis and to assemble a sales force of some kind. One of my first hires, I'm happy to report, was also my best: I persuaded Bernice to leave her position at Maremont Automotive to come and work for me. She wasn't crazy about the idea at first; I was only able to offer her one hundred dollars a week, which represented a substantial pay cut, but I like to think I was such a good salesman she couldn't help but come aboard. More likely, she felt if she was going to throw in with an upstart like me, she would do well to keep a close eye on the books, but I wasn't about to question her motives. I was just thrilled to have her. She really had a fine business sense, and I knew she would be an enormous asset going forward.

The first order of business was scouting new or poorly marketed regional products that I could introduce on a national scale.

Manufacturers would be only too happy to give me their business, I felt, because I offered a win-win situation. If I increased their sales and opened up new markets, I would participate only in the increased volume; if I couldn't move a product or make an appreciable difference, it wouldn't cost them a penny. Initially, I focused on the cosmetics and pharmaceutical industries because that was where my contacts were. I knew those businesses. I started representing Q-tips, which was a very small item at the time, and also a pharmaceutical item called Dolcin, which was an over-the-counter analgesic product. I also represented a line of bubble baths and, of course, Beauty Wave.

Slowly, I began to realize that to make a proper living and expand the company into a sizeable force, I needed to reach outside these industries for new products. With this in mind, I made a trip to New York to attend the annual toy fair, where all the toy, game, and doll manufacturers convened to display their wares and innovations. I wandered around the convention floor, looking for something unusual, something I could possibly take to my chain and drug store contacts, when I spotted an intriguing paint-by-numbers set. The concept since has become a bellwether in the crafts industry, but, in the late 1940s, few people had seen the sets before. The product was simple: there was a line drawing on a white page with numbers corresponding to different colors on a paint palette. You brushed on the paint according to the numbers on the page, and you wound up with a picture. It really was a clever notion. There were simple drawings for children to paint and sophisticated replicas of famous paintings for adults to follow. What excited me about it was that it was completely unlike the Beauty Wave kits, and yet I could draw on some of the same store contacts to sell it. I reached out to the manufacturers and arranged to represent the kits exclusively across the country to all the drug chains and department stores. In those days, supermarkets didn't carry novelty items such as these, although today, of course, there are whole aisles devoted to toys, books, and games.

We sold those kits like crazy. I set up shop in an office building at 936 North Michigan Avenue, across from the Drake Hotel where Bernice and I were married. Quickly, I assembled a small sales force. I had a fellow in Los Angeles to cover the West Coast, a person in Chicago, one in Minneapolis, one in Detroit, one in New York, and so forth. Eventually, I increased the sales staff to fifteen, and I looked on each person as a fairly low-risk hire. A salesman looked to make his money in commissions, so if he didn't perform he didn't get paid. There were expenses to be covered, to be sure, and, in some cases, there were stipend arrangements, but for the most part, the sales staff paid for itself. In those days, all of our selling was done face to face, so it was important to have a presence in each region of the country. You could do your follow-up calls over the telephone, but it was necessary to establish these important relationships in person. That was the way business got done, and this was never more apparent than in our quick success with this paint-by-numbers item. Goodness, we couldn't service the accounts fast enough, that's how popular these items became. We put together a display rack that held eight or ten kits, and each rack unit represented about a fifty-dollar sale; we collected 10 percent for our efforts. It turned out to be a tremendous windfall for our young company. All of a sudden, we started getting commission checks for three, four, sometimes five thousand dollars a month—just from this one item! That was a lot of money back then; it's a lot of money, still.

Here, as with all the new items I was carrying, I patterned my approach after the successful systems we'd put in place for the home permanent kits. We initially reached into targeted markets of a certain size and then followed up these efforts with a more ongoing campaign. We offered co-op advertising. And, we were determined to become the market leader in each product category.

I remember moving these paint-by-numbers kits by the carload to places like Walgreens and Thrifty on the West Coast, and a now-defunct chain called Whelans in New York. After a while of this, the manufacturer got a little heady with success and determined to step up production. What it meant for us was a certain pressure to distribute even more aggressively, which led me to my first lesson in managing the strain of too much of a good thing. We had to ask our accounts to double-up on their orders or, in some cases, to take three or four times their usual amount in order to satisfy the manufacturer. It meant that we had to give dating to some of our smaller accounts. To "date" an order meant that the buyer did not have to pay for it for sixty days, which can be a worrisome thing. On an isolated basis, you can get away with it here and there, especially for a good account of long standing. But we wrote some big orders for brand new accounts, and there were all kinds of monies tied up in credit. We reached a critical point where I became concerned for the flow of our commissions. I was afraid the manufacturer would run out of money; if they had so much tied up in inventory, and so much tied up in dating, there would be nothing left for us.

Initially, I was able to make a deal with the manufacturer to receive our commission checks every week instead of every month, but, soon enough, the checks stopped coming. The manufacturer went bust, and our good run was over—but not before we made a small fortune on the item. We may have lost out on a couple months of commissions, but, on balance, we did extremely well on the deal. And I learned to never let dollar signs cloud my vision to the point that supply outpaces demand. I learned it the hard way, at significant cost, but I prided myself on never making the same mistake twice.

⁂

Despite our early success, we were still a bare-bones operation. The beautiful thing about a national sales company like ours was that it didn't need to grow beyond a certain point. Or, I should say, I didn't need to expand the sales force in order to increase sales. Our growth came in new product lines, and not in personnel. An aggressive salesman could peddle several items on a single sales call, so there was tremendous promise. There was also room for growth in acquisition, and when I couldn't come to terms with a manufacturer on representation for a product, I sometimes looked to buy the product outright to add it to our line in that way. In fact, I went back to Frank Hall after I had some success with my sales operation and inquired about the Beauty Wave kits. He was retired by this time, but the business was still going. It wasn't what it had been, but it was a solvent company, and I felt there was still some life in the product, so I took it on.

It was a remarkable turn, to be able to come back to the place where I had gotten my start and buy out my former boss, but I tried not to let my emotions get in the way of the transaction. It was a good deal, done on pleasant, equitable terms; Frank Hall wasn't doing much with the product, and I felt we could do more.

And we did, after a time. We made a number of additional product line purchases in much the same way over the next few months, such as Enoz, a line of moth cakes and flakes purchased from Diversey Chemical. Overall, we fairly thrived. We bought inventory, patents, and manufacturing equipment—whatever it took to continue production. Sometimes, we took over office or factory space if it made good economic sense. Bernice kept the books for us, and she couldn't have been more pleased with how our little company was performing. I looked over her shoulder and shared her enthusiasm.

At some point early on in this enterprise, I met a Swiss cosmetic chemist who worked for a Chicago-based company called Lady Esther. Lady Esther was a boutique operation that managed to compete successfully with larger outfits like Elizabeth Arden. From time to time, I met employees of companies like Lady Esther who had an entrepreneurial streak of their own. This fellow's name was Jules Montenier, and he had learned how to "blowmold" plastic bottles. He called me into his lab one afternoon and showed me what he was able to do. In those days, I was always thinking, always scheming. My idle thoughts turned invariably to cosmetics, perfumes, or other personal products with which I now had become professionally familiar. One of the great puzzles to me, at that time, was the way antiperspirant was only available in cream form. I thought that if someone came up with a way to dispense an antiperspirant without such mess, fuss, or bother, they would have a winner. So I asked this chemist if he thought he could put a deodorant or antiperspirant in his bottles. He said he needed to think about it for a while. Wouldn't you know it, a week or so later, he called me up and asked me to stop by his office at my earliest convenience.

Well, this Mr. Montenier was a few steps ahead of me by the time I arrived. He unveiled a plastic squeeze bottle, which he had filled with a deodorant solution. To my thinking, the deodorant it-self wasn't nearly as important as the way it would be dispensed. Sometimes, a production revolution comes in the packaging or design before it comes from product performance.

"I've already registered the idea, Mr. Lavin," this Montenier fellow announced proudly. "I'm going to call it Stopette."

I liked the name and the idea. I didn't much like that he'd gone out and registered the thing on his own, but I still saw it as an opportunity. "Could you make the bottle in a smaller size?" I asked.

"I could make it whatever size we want," he said.

At this, I suggested he consider manufacturing the item in a value size, which could retail for $1.25, and a small size, which could retail for sixty cents. I had no idea if the darn stuff worked, but I loved the concept. I felt sure that the American public would love it, too. The deodorant creams on the market were so messy and uncomfortable that people would clamor for something bet-ter to pat under their arms. I didn't care how far along this Mr. Montenier was in his product development, I wanted in, so I rolled up my sleeves and made him an offer.

"You need national representation," I announced, with quiet confidence. "I'd be willing to take you on, that is, if you want me to. Say, a fifty-fifty split, all down the line. You handle the man-ufacturing, and I'll handle the selling and the advertising. I'll even buy the finished goods from you at ten percent above cost, so that you can make that extra profit as well."

Mr. Montenier thought about this for a bit, but he was not a businessman. He was a chemist, an inventor. It was, I thought, a fair deal for both sides. To my thinking, there's no profit in forging a partnership on onerous terms. In order for a business relationship to thrive, it must be built on a foundation of trust and reason. I used to think, when I was just starting out, that it paid to strike a deal that offered my partners as much as I could possibly afford, as opposed to as little as I could get away with. It made good business sense. I believed then, and still do believe, in being generous with partners because in runaway success, there is usually enough money to go around no matter how you slice it. This was especially so in the case of this antiperspirant, considering my hoped-for partner had no experience bringing his product to the marketplace. He needed someone to watch his back and his bottom line, and it wouldn't do to enter into a business arrangement with a fellow like that where he might be made to feel mistrust on any level.

We would be partners, I proposed, in every sense. Plain and simple. He considered my terms carefully, and, after a beat or two, he smiled and we shook hands on it. Now, it was left to me to figure a way to make good on my claims and sell the heck out of this product. If things fell our way, I knew that the underarm deodorant would be just the foundation for which I was looking.

# 3

## The Power of Television

IN THE EARLY 1950S, THE LANDSCAPE OF AMERICAN MARKETING changed. Actually, it didn't just change, it transformed. In fact, it's fair to say that over a fairly short stretch of time, from, say, 1949 to 1953, the way products were sold in this country was completely reinvented. We went from being a vast nation, where word-of-mouth, traveling salesmen, and regional print and radio broadcast advertising were the only resources available to manufacturers and distributors, to being a small, accessible national community, linked by the most powerful advertising and marketing tool in the history of mankind.

That tool, for good or ill, was television—and the Leonard H. Lavin Sales Co. was all over it.

Indulge me, readers, in a small digression before I examine the impact of the medium on our marketing efforts, and the impact of our marketing efforts on the medium. You see, I long have believed that television played an integral part in our development as a company, just as we might have played at least a small part in the evolution of the broadcasting industry. The following brief aside nicely illustrates the connection.

Early on in our marriage, Bernice and I found the time and the resources to sneak in a wonderful vacation in Hawaii. We loved to stay in the penthouse at the Surfrider on Oahu, and, one afternoon, I returned from a round of golf to find Bernice walking with two men on the beach. It turned out that they were David Sarnoff, "the General," who was the head of RCA, the parent company of NBC, and Walter Kaiser, the noted industrialist, who was in Hawaii building Kaiser Village, which is now known as the Hilton Hawaiian Village. Leave it to my wife to attract the attention of such movers and shakers. As I joined the group for their walk on the beach, General Sarnoff recognized my name because, even then, I was a fairly prominent advertiser on network television. We shared some stories about the industry and some common friends, and the afternoon turned into a dinner.

At one point during the dinner, General Sarnoff asked me what I would like to see different about television. I had several ideas, but one of them was that we could sell beauty products much more effectively if we could show both the models and the packages in color. The General nodded in agreement, and the conversation moved on to another topic.

Over the years, we maintained this island-based association, and we often met for dinner when we found ourselves in the same city. Two or three years after this initial conversation, the General asked Bernice what kind of furniture we had in our home. She thought it an odd question, but replied that is was a simple collection, in no particular style. A couple weeks later, a deliveryman appeared at our door with two gorgeous color television sets (and remember, televisions at that time were major pieces of furniture)—one in blonde wood and one in mahogany. A note attached simply said, "Thanks, from General Sarnoff."

Of course, I'm not so brazen to suggest that I invented color television, or even that I had a hand in its conception, but I like to think I spurred its development some.

Now, on to a more substantive account. Our first major, national television campaign, for Stopette, offered a blueprint for all of our future television advertising efforts. I learned that aspect of the business as I went along in much the same way I learned other aspects of the business up until this time. I made mistakes. I tried new things. I worked to understand the big picture and bring it down to size. In this, I suppose, I was like every other upstart businessman looking to get a leg up on his bottom line. The great promise of advertising in such an exciting new medium was too rich to ignore, and if we stumbled along the way, that was just the cost of doing business in this new manner. After all, it is reasonable and expected to make a mistake once; to make the same mistake a second time . . . well, then you might want to consider another line of work.

When we were ready to introduce our new antiperspirant, there was no such thing as a truly national television network. What there was, in the main, was a loosely linked consortium of independently owned stations offering programming provided by the parent network. It *seemed* like a network and *acted* like a network. It even called itself a network. But it wasn't a network like we know the term today. In 1950, when we were looking to launch Stopette, there were only a dozen or so cities airing national programming on a synchronized schedule. Individual stations owners were encouraged to carry a network feed live, as it happened, but much of the schedule was kept open for local programming. Independent stations were also free to carry their own programming or taped programming in place of network fare if they didn't feel the network offering would attract an audience in their market. In Milwaukee, for example, where the CBS affiliate station was owned by the same company that published the *Milwaukee Journal*, the station manager wasn't much interested in carrying a program sponsored by an underarm product. It didn't matter that the show we'd chosen to sponsor was one of the most popular programs on television at the time; it mattered that someone in the station's front office felt it was a shade unseemly to be peddling antiperspirant on its airwaves.

Who could argue with that kind of backward thinking? Of course, one of the staples on television in those days was local wrestling shows, a tame precursor to the popular WWE wrestling shows of today. You'd think a deodorant commercial would fit right into the mix, but, from time to time, we looked for something a bit more highbrow to showcase our product. We did plenty of advertising on wrestling shows, however. Indeed, our very first buys were regional wrestling programs, but I longed to associate our product with top-tier programs when I could afford it.

Going back to the Milwaukee example cited above, the show in question was the popular quiz show, *What's My Line?* For a stretch of time during the 1950s, it was one of the most successful programs on the air. It ran for more than seventeen years, and, in that time, it helped to sell a lot of antiperspirant, the Milwaukee station notwithstanding. (Incidentally, the stuffed-shirt Milwaukee station manager eventually relented and began carrying *What's My Line?* some time later, even with our onerous deodorant ads. At which point, it was noted, Milwaukee residents began to smell a whole lot better.)

The *What's My Line?* concept was simple: there was a panel of four celebrities charged with discovering the job or identity of a certain mystery guest. Panelists could ask only *yes* or *no* questions, as in the popular game of Twenty Questions, and contestants were awarded money or prizes each time a question yielded an answer of no. Panelists sometimes were blindfolded to keep them from guessing the identity of the mystery guest, or the guest was kept behind a partition of some kind, visible to the home viewer, but not to the other participants on stage.

Stopette was one of the first sponsors of the program, and it was a good association all around. Of course, we didn't jump into this type of national advertising campaign with both feet. We tried it first in local, targeted markets. We made the kind of tentative media buys we could afford on our limited budget. The regional wrestling shows actually were more affordable, so we made our early concentrated buys in this area. Those early wrestling shows didn't carry the bells and whistles and braggadocio of today, but they were certainly a lot less conservative than other types of programming on the dial. Boxing programs, too, represented a key portion of our initial advertising buys. The results were fantastic and immediate, so much so that we quickly suspended all other forms of advertising. Nothing else came close to television. We continued with our co-op advertising with local accounts around the country in newspapers and circulars because, of course, we had to in order to keep up those relationships. But we pulled out of radio and magazine advertising entirely, once we realized the cost-effectiveness of a well-placed, well-executed television spot.

Bernice and I went over our books each week and considered how much money we could afford to spend on advertising for the following week, right down to the very last dollar. We scraped by on a strict austerity budget, except when it applied to television. We somehow found the money to get our product out there and discussed. The strategy was to spend as much as we could afford, as opposed to as little as we could get away with. It was, I believed, the only course available to us. If there was money in our accounts, we put it to work on television because I felt strongly then, as I do today, that there is no better way to push a product; idle funds always can be put to aggressive use. When I calculated that we could stretch our dollars farther on something other than a regional wrestling show, I looked to the CBS lineup of shows to see if there was a program we could sponsor outright.

As it turned out, CBS chief Bill Paley was a distant cousin of mine, although neither one of us was aware of the family connection at the time. His father and my great-grandfather started out in Chicago together, rolling cigars, and, at some point, the Paley line moved on to New York, where they rolled their cigar stake into a small radio station and began to build a broadcasting empire. We eventually became good friends over the course of our years-long association with the network, but, in those early days, he didn't know me from a hole in the wall, and I didn't know him, either. It took my grandmother to point out the family tie.

I don't mean to pass myself off as a visionary or a wizened entrepreneur because, in truth, I was neither in those days. I was simply a seat-of-the-pants businessman willing to try something new because I didn't feel I could compete on a national scale by the conventional business model. And the early days of television were anything but conventional. I came across the *What's My Line?* program quite by accident. Bernice and I enjoyed watching it when it came on each week, but it never occurred to me to advertise on it until someone from CBS mentioned there was a sponsorship opening on the program. The show was sponsored by the Toni company, a manufacturer of hair care products, but the Toni people didn't feel committed enough to the medium, or deeppocketed enough to carry the entire program, so we agreed to split the arrangement with them. It was an unusual setup, but it made it affordable for a company like ours. The way it worked was we alternated from one week to the next. We had our signage up on the stage during the Stopette weeks and copy written for the host, John Daly, to read at various points during the broadcast. We even produced our own black and white commercials to air throughout the program. And it was a very profitable association. Our product moved like crazy, with unprecedented velocity, the morning after each of our *What's My Line?* programs aired, and I sat with Bernice and "Doc," as our Mr. Montenier came to be known, to marvel at our good fortune at thinking to promote our product in this new way.

A few months into this profitable relationship, the brass at CBS decided to move *What's My Line?* from its mid-week time slot to Sunday nights, and this was seen as a great upheaval in the advertising community. In retrospect, it really was a small matter, but back then it was a real concern. See, up until this time, Sunday nights had been a kind of uncertain position for advertisers looking to promote their products. Ed Sullivan's *Toast of the Town* aired on Sunday nights on CBS, of course, and it was one of the most popular programs on the air. But there was a general feeling that American people was less open to sales pitches on Sundays, when stores were generally closed, than they were during the week. It was even felt that certain product categories, such as personal hair care or hygiene products, would move better on other evenings. This may or may not have been true, but frankly I didn't much care. I liked being associated with a smart, witty, successful, urbane program like *What's My Line?* and was only too happy to continue that association on a new night, even if that night fell on a Sunday.

It was a risk, to be sure, but it was a risk worth taking. Permit me, please, a horse-playing analogy: if you're prepared to bet on a horse, you'll like him coming out of the eighth position almost as much as you'll like him coming out of the first gate. (It is, I'll allow, a flawed analogy because there are some horses you *only* like coming out of the inside gate, but I believe I've made my point.)

The Toni folks, however, felt somewhat differently—all horse racing references aside—and when they backed out of the program, we took the entire sponsorship on ourselves. It was a stretch for us to make that kind of financial commitment, but I felt the upside to such tremendous exposure was too rich to ignore. Plus, I didn't want Stopette to have to share the stage any longer with another product. (Who knew what product CBS would bring in alongside ours?) Let *What's My Line?* be known as the Stopette show, I thought, and let's see what happens.

What happened next was spurred along by the biggest, and some would say most frivolous, expense of my young career. I've always thought the money was well spent and a sound investment in our all-important relationships with buyers around the country and network and advertising executives in New York, but I will admit that I choked a bit when I received the final tab. I decided to throw a party, a fantastically big, pull-out-the-stops party to celebrate our sole sponsorship of the program and to let our various people know that we meant to be a significant player on the national scene. What's the old saying, it takes money to make money? Well, here it took a *lot* of money. And then a little bit more besides.

The idea was to bring our entire sales force and all the buyers from around the country into New York to sit in the studio audience during one of the first Sunday night broadcasts of *What's My Line?* There were some key accounts, some really big drug store chains, upon which we depended to place and push our deodorant; television was new enough and exciting enough that a trip to New York to see behind the scenes was a great big deal to some of the buyers and store owners. Plus, the chance to mix and mingle with television celebrities was as enticing in 1951 as it is today, and the *What's My Line?* panel had quickly become household names and faces. There was the actress Arlene Francis, syndicated columnist Dorothy Kilgallen, writer Hal Block, historian Louis Untermeyer, and the host of the program, newsman John Daly, who also served as anchor of ABC's nightly news broadcasts.

We invited everyone to bring their spouses or significant others. The logistical dilemma was that all these people were spread out all over the country. So I arranged for them to come into Chicago, and we departed together on board the Twentieth Century Limited train to New York. I booked two entire sections of the train for our party, and that's exactly what it was for the half-day or so it took to cross to New York—a party on a grand scale. We had sleeping cars and club cars, and there was drinking and dancing and merry-making of all kinds. I must say, it truly was quite a trip, with no expense spared, and once we arrived at Grand Central Station, there was a fleet of limousines to ferry us to the Waldorf-Astoria Hotel, where I had booked a couple of floors. There, the party continued. By Sunday evening, our group had spilled to the CBS studios, and we sat and watched the show. It was a marvelous thing, and the mood of our crowd was boisterous and infectious. John Daly joined in on some of our good times before the broadcast, and I don't mean to be indecorous, but he was a bit wobbly on his feet as the evening progressed. Just as the show was about to go on the air, he was fairly staggering. At times, he had to reach out to keep himself from falling. Something obviously was amiss with him, but he was a true professional. He sat down at his desk on stage, the hot lights went on, and he delivered his lines without a hitch. It was the most remarkable thing, almost magical, the way he sat up suddenly straight and went into his introduction. And when he read the lines of the Stopette copy, it sounded to this would-be deodorant mogul as if Daly were quoting scripture!

The entire weekend was a grand success. The actress Gloria Swanson was the mystery guest on the program, and she was kind enough to join us following the show. This was a tremendous hit among the wives of our group. They were all just so thrilled to be in such grand company, on such equal footing. It was a sensational bash for a modest man like me to throw, but we all felt it was a worthwhile expense, one that would bring us a substantial return in the years to come. Whether or not it did, I could never be sure, but it certainly paid dividends.

The price tag I choked on? About one hundred thousand dollars for the airfares, the train tickets, the hotels, and all the food, drink, and whatnot—even today, it is an awful lot of money for a shindig. Back then, it was just about sinful, but that was what it took to get us noticed.

And the Sunday night time slot was also a hit. Advertisers realized that goods and services peddled on this day of rest had the same shot at attention as those offered on other evenings, and, as the sole sponsor of a hit show, we had the nation's undivided attention. Truly, our deodorant just flew off the shelves each Monday morning, and there was a direct correlation to the success of the show the night before. The more people tuned in, the more they bought our merchandise; you actually could chart the ratings against our sales. I felt that we rolled the dice and came up a real winner.

Some months into this winning equation, our competitors introduced different types of antiperspirants dispensed in new ways, and there was one method that seemed worthy of our attention. At this point, we were the clear market leader in the category, but I never was content to rest on our reputation; if the competition could go back to the drawing boards for something new, then so could the Leonard H. Lavin Sales Co. I went to see Dr. Montenier one afternoon and asked him if he could figure a way to create a hairspray in an aerosol can; the sprays seemed to be the next big thing in the industry, and I didn't want to be caught short.

"Leonard," he said, with a thick Swiss-French accent, "I am a plastic man. I am not an aerosol man." There was a lilt to his voice that made everything he said sound like a question: *I am not an aerosol man?*

I didn't see how this had anything to do with whether or not he could *become* an aerosol man so that we could *become* an aerosol product, but Monty could stand firm on a point. And so, we were a little slow on the aerosol front while my stubborn partner remained a plastic man. We were still a market leader, so I couldn't complain, but that didn't stop Dr. Montenier from developing an issue or two. At one point, well into our established success with Stopette, he approached me one afternoon and indicated that I was making too much money off his product, his innovation, and his expertise. This took me somewhat by surprise, although, on balance, the difficulty worked out in my favor, as I will explain.

"What do you mean, Doctor?" I shot back. "I'm making just as much as you. In fact, you're making a little extra because you get that 10 percent bump on production."

"Yes, but I developed this product," he answered. "I developed the plastic bottle. It's my name and my face in our advertising. I've done everything."

I had no ready response to a charge like this, but I told Doc I would have to think about things. I never liked to respond to an unexpected turn of events without first having a chance to sort the situation out in my head to look at all the related scenarios, so I kept my mouth shut. I could have countered that I built the product, made it a household name, and gave it far more prominence and profitability than Doc could have managed on his own, but I chose not to do so. If there's one thing I can't abide as a businessman, it's being in partnership with someone who thinks he's getting screwed—especially after you've gone out of your way to ensure a fair deal.

And so I thought about it, and this was what I came up with: I had to buy Doc out or he had to buy me out. Either way, the partnership could not continue now that he had introduced the notion of mistrust or disadvantage. I told Doc that it was up to him to decide how to dissolve the partnership. I would go along with whatever he decided. He felt strongly that it was *his* product, *his* creativity, and *his* proprietary interests on the line, so I left it to him. In the back of my mind, I knew he never would let me buy him out of his interest because, in our advertising, he became the public face of our product. He was the genius behind Stopette, a celebrity in his own right, deep into his fifteen minutes of fame. But our Mr. Montenier really seemed to relish all that publicity. I couldn't see him giving that up. And, indeed, he couldn't either.

Ultimately, he agreed to buy out my interest in the product, and I was fortunate that Monty's greed coincided with the height of Stopette's market dominance. Maybe it had to do with me stepping away from the marketing effort, or maybe it had to do with the competition finally catching up to our bright ideas, but I cashed out at just the right time, just as poor Mr. Montenier's avarice got the better of him at precisely the wrong time in our sales history.

Stopette had a great run, but it ran its course. I returned to the Leonard H. Lavin Sales Co. and redoubled my efforts to uncover the next great American selling opportunity. With all of this hard-won experience in the television and advertising games, I felt I was well positioned to make another run with the right product in the right market. And, with a generous settlement from my Stopette interests, I increased my all-important "foundation money" until I was well positioned to buy into my next opportunity.

All I had to do was find it.

# 4

# Five Vital Oils

I CONSIDERED MYSELF EXTREMELY FORTUNATE TO HAVE PARLAYED A new concept into a runaway, market-leading success like Stopette, and I reminded myself that every good run came to an end. That one may have run out on me sooner than I liked, but it nevertheless had been a profitable enterprise.

And it wasn't just the kind of profit that could be counted and socked away as capital or foundation money. No, there was tremendous profit in the wealth of experience and contacts I gleaned along the way. Not least among these, of course, was the crash course I gave myself in television advertising, and it saved me all sorts of time on our next product launch. But equally important were the many buyers and representatives all across the country, many of whom became good friends through our lucrative association. (Trust me: there's nothing like a good deal all around for building key business relationships.) I spoke to a couple dozen of these good people every day as I returned my efforts to my national sales company, and, on each call, I made a point of asking if they'd come across anything new or exciting since the last time we'd spoken. This was my way of keeping my ear to the ground long distance, and it was a practice that defined my career going forward; I always listened for news of some underperforming product or new idea.

It was in this way, in fact, that I came across the product around which I built the balance of my career, and upon which I built a brand and a corporation. I was on the West Coast scouring area drug stores on behalf of some of the new lines I was selling, seeing what I could see, and lunching with Bob Borun, the president of the Thrifty drug chain. At the time, in the middle 1950s, Thrifty was a fairly large regional drug chain, comparable to a Walgreens. Really, in terms of our business, it was huge, and Bob Borun long had been an important account and a good and trusted friend. What I trusted most about Bob were his instincts. He was like me in this way, with a knack for spotting an interesting trend. "Is there anything new, Bob?" I asked him during our lunch. "Anything I haven't seen?"

"Well, Leonard," he said, "funny you should ask."

I don't know why he found it funny because I asked him all the time, but, on this day, he had something to tell me. It seemed that there was a product that caught his attention for the way it moved solely on customer word-of-mouth. There was no advertising for it and no prominent in-store display, but women came in and asked for it. He couldn't keep enough of the stuff in stock. He moved very big numbers for a single item. The product was a hairdressing and conditioner that seemed to be favored by the Hollywood community and was carried by virtually every West Coast beauty salon. It was said to be popular among movie studio hairstylists for the way it kept the stars' hair looking stylish and manageable under the hot lights. Those lights were brutal on a beautiful head of hair, hour after hour after hour, and this product was designed to leave hair looking shiny, moisturized, and full of body, even after a full day on the set. Word got around, and pretty soon every woman in town had to have her own tube of the stuff. Yet, the company did no advertising to support the product. Not only that, but the entire Thrifty chain had never seen a salesman. Bob kept the product in stock because his customers kept asking for it, but no one came around to get him to up his order or anything like that. The thing fairly sold itself.

Bob told me the name of the product, and I had to laugh: Alberto VO5. It struck me as a funny name. I had never heard of it before, naturally, and it was sold in a fairly inconspicuous package. I took one look at the name and the packaging and had a good long chuckle. I thought, here I was, beating my head against the wall, spending money on advertising, product development, and package design for all these various lines, and a thing like this comes along and just flies off the shelves.

What the heck did I know?

Well, I knew enough to ask a few questions. According to Bob Borun, the fellow who owned the company recently had taken ill and was looking to sell the business and get his affairs in order. I hated to hear of an opportunity that grew out of someone else's misfortune, but if this gentleman was determined to sell, perhaps I could help him achieve a fair price if it made good business sense. I had Bob make an introductory call right away, and he put me on the phone.

The fellow's name was Hoffman, and he confirmed that he was looking to sell his company, so I asked if I could come out to see him to discuss the matter. I thought that as long as I was in Los Angeles, I would try to arrange a meeting with him, and, happily, Mr. Hoffman was free that evening. He invited me to his house for dinner, and we spent several hours discussing the Alberto VO5 product and a few of his other lines as well. Before I went, I thought I ought to try the product for myself to see what all the fuss was about, and it worked pretty well. It was pleasant and easy to use, and it kept my hair looking neat and full. I have very dry hair, and this stuff was so highly concentrated that I only took the tiniest drop. I worked it into my hair and combed it out, and it left me with very nice sheen and manageability. I'd never used a product like it in my life to that point, but I've used it every day since.

For his part, in preparation, Mr. Hoffman got his profit and loss statement for me to inspect between the time of our phone call and the time of our meeting, and I must admit the numbers looked good. I suppose it's easy to have good-looking numbers when your principle product sells itself, but then again *that* was why I was interested in the business.

Mr. Hoffman told me the history of his company, which he called the Alberto-Culver Company, and I found it interesting. I never knew how much of the history was apocryphal, but, to tell the truth, I never bothered to check any of the information. A good story was a good story, and I chose early on to let this one stand. The founder of the company was a man named Blaine Culver, and, according to Mr. Hoffman, this Culver fellow hired a chemist with a first name of Alberto to help him develop his flagship product. Before stumbling across the Alberto VO5 formula, Mr. Culver was mostly a manufacturer and distributor of salon-based products, which he, in fact, sold mostly to area salons. He didn't exactly shoot for the moon in his business plan. His biggest customers worked in Hollywood's film and television studios. According to legend, as he walked through one of the studios on a sales call, Mr. Culver was approached by several veteran stylists. They asked if he had ever come across a styling product that would be gentle on hair underneath the hot studio lights. Good salesman that he was, Mr. Culver replied that he had just the thing, even though he didn't have the first idea. One of the stylists asked him to bring a half-pound jar of the stuff with his next order so that he could try it out. So, Mr. Culver went home and started thinking, and what he thought to do was to consult a chemist. He hired Alberto, who developed the Alberto VO5 formula, and they were in business. It's essentially the same formula we use today because when you stumble across a thing that works, you stay with it.

I still thought it was a funny name, but Mr. Hoffman explained to me that it stood for five vital oils. Nobody ever was sure exactly what the name stood for because, in a holdover from World War II, Mr. Culver was prohibited by the government from using the word "vital" in his packaging, just as we later were prohibited from using it in our advertising. I never understood that restriction, but we were made to live with it. There was a certain logic behind it, I suppose, but it seemed clear in this case that we weren't passing this product off as "vital" in the literal sense. It wasn't as if regular use of our hairdressing was crucial to the health and well-being of our customers; it merely was crucial to the health and well-being of our business.

At some point, Mr. Hoffman took over the operation from Mr. Culver, and he continued to produce and market the hairdressing under its original name. Understand, I use the term "market" fairly loosely here because there wasn't much marketing going on when I came on the scene, but the product was, nevertheless, a strong regional seller. There were a couple hundred other products in Hoffman's inventory in addition to the Alberto VO5, but I wasn't much interested in them. The trouble was, he wanted to sell the whole lot of them in a kind of package deal, so I built a model around what made sense for the one product, thinking I might just kill off all those others once the deal was done. All told, the product line did about five hundred thousand dollars worth of business, so I offered Mr. Hoffman a price that roughly corresponded to a dollar-for-dollar deal in terms of sales. Five hundred thousand dollars seemed about right for a company of that size at that time. Plus, I offered dollar-for-dollar for existing inventory, which amounted to another several thousand dollars. My plan was to relocate the business back to Chicago, quickly to drop those other products once I determined whether or not they performed, and to concentrate on this unique hairdressing item.

Mr. Hoffman agreed to the terms on good faith, and I conducted the follow-through with a due-diligence I probably should have undertaken before making the offer, but I was so convinced of the value of this one particular product. At the time of our proposed transaction, the entire Alberto-Culver operation was run out of a tiny storefront in Los Angeles. The plant and warehouse facility was about the size of a dry cleaning store, and Mr. Hoffman had a little setup out back where he mixed the product by hand in big empty oil drums. There was a small patio, I recall, and this was where he stored the big oil drums. It wasn't exactly a sophisticated factory operation, but it was enough to meet the limited demand. There was a hand-operated tube-filling machine, which was used to fill each tube one at a time; it was a slow process, which didn't seem to aggravate Mr. Hoffman nearly as much as it bothered me. I could never run a business in such a jury-rigged way.

I learned the entire business in a matter of days—Mr. Hoffman passed on the formula to me, as it were—and I returned to Chicago to arrange for financing. I had my seed money in place, which, by then, was nearly enough to pay for the whole deal outright, but I wasn't going to disturb it if I didn't have to do so. I'd taken Frank Hall's advice to heart, and I meant to increase those monies into a formidable safety net. Instead, I looked to a group of investors who came into my acquaintance; these men had an expressed interest in the cosmetics industry and considerable monies at their disposal. I thought they'd spark to an opportunity like this. I also thought it was better to put their money to work on the idea instead of mine.

Let me first share the story of how I met these good people because I think it's instructive. Bernice and I traveled on business to a convention, and I always made a point of milling about and meeting new people in these like-minded business environments. I worked on the supposition that you never knew who you might run into and who might be in a position to help you in one way or another at one point or another. In business, contacts are key, and it is only with diligence and an outgoing personality that you can build a viable network of such acquaintances. And so, when our flight was delayed, I drifted toward a pleasant fellow seated next to me in the waiting area and struck up a conversation. It was apparent from the man's demeanor that he hadn't done much traveling (in those days, a trip on an airplane was still beyond the means or the needs of most people), so it was easy to find an entry-point of conversation. Our flight was delayed, so we talked about possible alternative travel plans, should our flight be canceled. I was traveling with Bernice, who was always on top of such matters, and she already had inquired about switching our tickets to another airline, so I suggested to this gentleman that he do the same. The gentleman's name was F.E. McCabe, and he let on that he was the chief financial officer for a rather large insurance company. He took my suggestion and got himself a seat on the same flight to which Bernice and I managed to switch. Actually, we wound up sitting together on the flight, and we had a very enjoyable conversation, after which we exchanged telephone numbers and such, and promised to keep in contact.

In those days, such a promise was no idle pledge. People in business, especially young people just starting out, made it a point to cultivate these relationships, and, in this, McCabe and I were cut from the same cloth. These days, everything happens so fast, and everyone seems to be out for himself; it's no longer clear how these all-important contacts get made. But things were different in the early 1950s, and McCabe and I got to be on very friendly terms and spoke frequently on the telephone. One afternoon, I got a call from him asking if he could come by with two of his partners for a meeting. They wanted to discuss a cosmetics item they'd invested in, and he knew I had some expertise in this area, so I told him I'd be happy to make the time.

He showed up the next afternoon with his two partners, W. Clement Stone, a major insurance company executive, and Illinois state senator W. Russell Arrington. These men had purchased an interest in a rather unique lipstick device that was unusual mostly for the way it dispensed the product, and they already had sunk a great deal of money into the thing. They wanted to know where to take it going forward. None of them were looking to get into the cosmetics business in anything but this sideline way, but all three clearly held a fierce entrepreneurial streak. They'd come up with a brush-like device that allowed the lipstick to be painted or brushed on, and they felt that there was great opportunity here. They were looking for advice and product representation, so I told them I would hold off on the advice until I had a chance to test the product in the marketplace. I held off on committing to take on the item as a sales representative until I had some indication of how it might perform. There was no sales volume to speak of at this point, so it was going to be fairly easy to measure the results of my efforts. I agreed to take it on as a consultant for a modest fee, and for three months I tried to gauge the demand for this item. Regrettably, there was none. Women found that the brush applied the lipstick in a very uneven, blotchy manner, and they weren't much interested in the item. So I called up McCabe and asked for a meeting.

"Gentlemen," I announced, in no uncertain terms. "I don't believe this product has the appeal to women that you all thought it would have going in." I didn't believe in hemming and hawing around the issue. The lipstick was a bust, and these people deserved the truth.

"But Leonard," one of them pushed, "our sales are up significantly since you've taken it on."

"That's true," I allowed, "but we were starting from virtually nothing, and with all the money I've got you pouring into advertising, sales should be far stronger. Plus, our research shows that customers just don't care for the item."

At this, the three partners looked at each other and took turns shrugging their shoulders. For a while, I didn't know if they were about to storm out in a huff, light into me for failing to position the thing properly, or what. Finally, Senator Arrington spoke. He was a shrewd man, whose reputation preceded him; as president *pro-tem* of the Illinois state senate, he was known as a decent but savvy negotiator and as an intelligent attorney. He told me how much he and his partners appreciated my honesty. He said I could have conned them along, and conned them along, and continued to collect a consulting fee for my efforts, milking it for all it was worth. But here I encouraged them to cut their losses and move on, thereby cutting myself out of a potential revenue stream in the bargain. "It's not every day you can get such good advice, Leonard," he said.

"Well," I said, "there's no point in beating a dead horse."

And, indeed, there wasn't.

After such as that, McCabe, Stone, Arrington, and I remained on very good terms, and when the opportunity to buy this hairdressing item came along, I thought of them. I could have gone to the bank and borrowed the money myself, but I felt the thing to do was arrange the deal on someone else's dime, if I could somehow manage to do so, and therefore limit my exposure. In the years since, this has become such a popular investment strategy that it's even got a catchy name: other people's money or O.P.M., for short. But back then, this simply struck me as an efficient way to raise some capital, and this trio of investors struck me as a likely match for their interest in cosmetics items and their already-demonstrated entrepreneurial leanings.

I called up my friend McCabe and asked for a meeting with him and his partners. They were happy to come up and talk to me, given our positive professional association the first time around. I told them all about the Alberto VO5 product, the Hollywood studios, and the chemist. I told them how I'd agreed to buy the business for five hundred thousand dollars and how I planned to phase out all the other items except the hairdressing. "I believe it's got a lot of merit," I said. "They're currently doing about one hundred thousand dollars in sales with that product, strictly on a regional basis, with no advertising or promotion to speak of."

They were interested, to a man, but at this point it was still unclear why I had called them in, so I laid it out for them. "I would like you to be my partners," I said. "If you'll put up the five hundred thousand dollars, and whatever else I'll need in terms of inventory, I'll give you 25 percent of the business."

They knew from our past dealings that I was an honorable fellow and that if this was what I was offering, it was because it struck me as fair. I wasn't out to strike a partnership offering as little equity as possible in order to snare some financing; conversely, I was hoping to put up as much equity as I could afford.

At this early juncture, 25 percent seemed to me a fairly generous figure that still left me with enough of the pie to work with if I should have to strike other partnership arrangements as we got going.

Well, Senator Arrington seemed particularly interested in these terms, and the others soon joined him in his enthusiasm. By the time the meeting broke, we had a deal. I went back out to Los Angeles as soon as it was feasible to finalize the transaction, and Senator Arrington sent one of the lawyers in his firm to accompany me to help expedite matters. The fellow's name was Peer Pederson, and, since, he's become a very well-known attorney in the Chicago area. As Pederson and I sat with Mr. Hoffman to go over the final details, I got a rather strange telephone call from Senator Arrington and company back in Chicago. It seemed that McCabe, Stone, and Arrington also were looking to finance their end of the deal; they'd gone to the American National Bank, which is now part of the First National Bank of Chicago, looking for a loan. Senator Arrington said that the loan officer wanted to ask me a couple of questions.

"Leonard," this man said, a little too loudly for the telephone. "Are you sure about this thing? You know, your partners here, they've had some failures in the past. Are you sure you know what you're doing?"

"Sir," I answered back, trying not to laugh at this odd exchange, "all I can tell you is I'm in it myself. I believe in the product. I believe it's a good deal all around."

This seemed to satisfy the loan officer because he didn't say anything, and, after a couple beats of stone silence, Senator Arrington got back on the line. "I don't know what you said to him, Leonard," he said, "but it apparently worked. Congratulations. We've got the loan."

Well, I didn't know what I said to him either, but it was good to be in business with these good people.

There was, I should mention, another amusing story involving the financing of the Alberto-Culver purchase. I heard once more from that American National banker, who called me again soon after this initial conversation to discuss an important matter. He had what I thought was a crazy request. He wanted me to come down and sign the note his office had prepared to guarantee the loan monies to McCabe, Stone, and Arrington. I couldn't understand why they needed my signature. My signature had never been discussed; I wasn't a party to their loan. The Alberto-Culver Company and its assets were not in any way put up as any kind of collateral. To my thinking, that loan had nothing to do with me. My deal was with my three partners, and their deal was with the bank. McCabe, Stone, and Arrington planned to sign on to the loan personally, and now the bank wanted me to sign personally. One of the few solid pieces of business advice my father gave me, in addition to not betting on anything beyond your direct control, was to never sign anything personally. "You'll get burned," he warned me. "It'll come back to bite you, just like it did me." How it came back to bite him was never made entirely clear, but I took his point.

So there I was, torn by my father's sound advice and the out-of-nowhere expectation that I personally would sign on to this loan, as my three friends apparently had agreed to do. I didn't know how to approach the subject with McCabe, Stone, and Arrington, and I didn't know how to refuse the banker without sending up some kind of red flag, so I held my tongue for the time being, figuring a plan would come to me. And one did, before too terribly long. The banker wanted me to come down to his office on a particular day to sign the necessary papers, and it just so happened that the date that year happened to correspond on the Jewish calendar to Rosh Hashanah, the Jewish New Year. Now, for those of you unfamiliar with Rosh Hashanah, it is considered to be one of the holiest days of the year, and observant Jews traditionally refrain from working on this day. And so, observant Jew that I never quite was, I expressed my shock and indignation to the banker, that he would even suggest I come down to his office on such a holy day.

"It's against my religion," I declared, with great solemnity.

At this, the banker recanted, and, for some reason, the matter was dropped. Whether it was forgotten or set aside then later deemed superfluous never was made clear. McCabe, Stone, and Arrington signed on to the deal as planned, but after I invoked the "Rosh Hashanah clause," the banker decided he didn't need to bother me about this after all, and that was that.

The exchange reminded me of the hurry-up-and-wait mentality that informs much of American business and legal affairs. We always race to close a deal and to generate necessary paperwork, and, in the end, we sometimes make do with what's at hand. Here, the bank had the three signatures it needed, and when getting mine proved difficult, the banker in charge essentially forgot he'd asked for it in the first place. The deal was done, and we moved on.

We had a good thing going as we sat on the verge of an enormous opportunity, and I didn't want to push my luck.

---

Even though I offered Mr. Hoffman dollar for dollar on inventory, there was no significant inventory to speak of on the Alberto-Culver warehouse shelves. It came, all told, to less than thirty thousand dollars. There was even some petty cash laying around in company coffers, and I had to pay for it as well—thirty-three dollars of mine for thirty-three dollars of his, as I recall, which I thought was a fair (and fairly ludicrous) exchange.

I was anxious to get going with this Alberto VO5 product and excited for the opportunities it presented. You see, at the time, it was sold in virtually every beauty salon up and down the entire West Coast. There are more beauty salons in the country than there are drug stores, department stores, mass merchandisers, and supermarkets all put together, and I felt strongly that since these salons were using the product and recommending it to their customers, we were well positioned to roll out the product for retail sale. Already, with a bare-bones effort, the product was doing about one hundred thousand dollars in annual sales, so clearly there was tremendous room for growth. Remember, at the outset of this book, I suggested that I had an innate sense for unique items. Now my sense told me that I had sniffed out a winner. My backers in Chicago felt the same way, otherwise they wouldn't have been so quick to come up with the money to finance the purchase.

The plan, as we got going, was to kill off all of Alberto-Culver's other items one by one and to send out my few salesmen to try and build up the Alberto VO5 brand. I consulted with a local machine company on how to fill the aluminum tubes by machine, instead of by hand, which I felt would save us a good deal of money and manpower. We set up a small production line that immediately put the Los Angeles operation to shame. I purchased a number of high-quality kettles, which seemed to me a lot more professional than empty oil drums, and all kinds of other equipment. I found a decent space that could accommodate our production facility for the time being. Of course, it was nothing like our factory today, and nothing like it would soon become, but it was a start.

I hired a big German chemist named Dr. Schnell, who, over time, ran the production operation for us and developed formulas for new products. I'll always remember how he used to run around in that hot factory on hot summer days in nothing but his underwear. It was such an absurdly comical sight to see that great big bear of a man prance around our place of business in his skivvies, but it was so unbearably hot down there on the factory floor that we never begrudged him that small comfort, however out of place it seemed. He was always saying, in his heavy accent, "Yah, Mr. Lavin, we can do this much better if we try it this way," or somesuch. The man was constantly looking for new solutions to old problems.

Once, early on, I asked Dr. Schnell to come up with a "blue" version of our franchise hairdressing for our more senior customers with gray, white, or silver-blonde hair. He told me, "Yah, we can do this, never a problem." And sure enough, he came back a few days later with the same formula modified with a blue tint to help cover up the rusty look older people's hair sometimes gets. Now, I had a head of salt-and-pepper hair from a very early age. Whether I was turned prematurely gray by my stint in the war, or whether I worried too much over my business prospects, or whether it was simply a matter of genetics I never knew, but I was fairly far gone in this area by the time I met Bernice. I suppose it helped me in business because it made me look older and more distinguished (or so I was told), but I was always a little vain about it. I figured that if it troubled me, even a little bit, then it must trouble others as well. I don't know that this last is really ever the case, but that's the perception people have, and perceptions are often as important as the reality. In any event, I tried the sample Dr. Schnell offered and liked it immediately. In fact, to put a fine point on a claim I made earlier, it's the blue version of Alberto VO5 I've used every day since it's been available, and not the original formula. And so we began marketing this Alberto VO5 Blue to seniors—it highlights the gray, and makes it appear more vibrant—and it quickly accounted for 25 percent of our total volume. We produced one short "tag" commercial when the product first came out, but, after that, we never spent a penny on specific advertising or promotion. It's still held that 25 percent piece of the Alberto VO5 sales over the years.

But I don't mean to get ahead of the story. Our first order of business, beyond shedding these unwanted product lines, was to repackage the Alberto VO5 product for the national market. I consulted a professional design company and came up with a new logo and a handsome new look for our brand. I firmly believed that the design should reflect a unisex product because even though Alberto VO5 was sold almost exclusively to women at this point, I was betting that it would hold enormous appeal to men. After all, I used it. All of my friends started using it once I became involved, and everyone reported that his hair was more manageable, fuller, and better looking as a result. The advertising, though, continued to be aimed at women because my experience told me that it was women who bought these products for their households. Either they bought it for themselves or for their husbands, so the design had to be something a woman would be drawn to in the stores and a man would be comfortable using at home. And our thinking proved to be on the money because the design we came up with in 1955 is still the same, distinctive gold and black design we use today. Which takes me to another obvious theory of business: when you hit on a good thing, you stay with it. It is a theory which, I believe, has turned up on more than a few bumper stickers and T-shirts disguised as the catch-all phrase, "If it ain't broke, don't fix it."

The pricing we established to introduce the product was value-driven, even as we meant to position the hairdressing as a premium item. Our tubes came in one size, and we sold them for one dollar—a reasonable price point then as now. Along with the standard-sized tubes, we offered a free sample, which held enough hairdressing for several days' worth of styling. We told customers to try the sample package first; if they didn't like the product, they could bring back the unopened tube for a full refund. Happily, no one ever brought anything back. This was the case not only in Chicago, but all over the country. We also offered the hairdressing in a three-dollar jar, for our repeat customers. Today, just for comparison, these same size packages are sold for about $3.25 for the tube and about $7.00 dollars for the jar.

The slow going at the front end of our Alberto VO5 push had to do with our lack of working capital to manufacture, distribute, and promote the product. I'd tapped my investors, McCabe, Stone, and Arrington, for all I could at this early stage, so we had to roll out our first shipments on a shoestring. My sales force deployed some of the same strategies I used successfully to open up new markets for the Beauty Wave home permanent kits some years earlier. They got into the stores as quickly as possible with a minimum order, then let the product take off with word-of-mouth and customer testimonials. I bolstered this effort with some carefully placed advertising; we didn't have the money in those first weeks and months to cover the country with prime time television advertising as we did for Stopette, but we did buy some isolated commercial time on targeted programming. Most of our initial advertising was of the co-op variety in local newspapers around the country; we encouraged our new outlets to allow us to underwrite their advertising in circulars and such if they offered us an insert to their copy featuring the Alberto VO5 product and logo.

Our first television buy, for the record, was on a station in Philadelphia during daytime programming. It was just a local, one-time spot intended to boost sales and brand awareness in that one market, and I remember thinking how different this advertising effort was from the pull-out-the-stops Stopette campaign. I knew first-hand and full well the enormous power of television advertising, but we were handcuffed now by the enormous cost of the medium. Commercial time became far more expensive in the year since we had pulled out of Stopette, as networks expanded their reach across the country and more and more households bought television sets. For all our good prospects, we simply didn't have the money to make a concentrated television buy—and certainly not during the more expensive prime time hours. And so, we placed our ads where we could, whenever we could afford to do so. This type of spot-buying can be extremely successful, and it worked well for us right out of the gate, but I longed for the day when we could make an aggressive network buy and really give this product the kind of push it deserved.

That day came soon enough. Every dollar we generated in those first months went immediately back into the business. Money that came in from receivables went directly to payroll or accounts payable, and so on. There was no cushion to speak of, not for several months anyway, but midway into our first year with the product we began to see some great promise. It took some months, but we gradually achieved coast-to-coast distribution, and

I looked again to television advertising to increase our market share.

I never went to business school, but, from the very beginning, I was a self-taught student of various business models and practices. I developed one of my own to help chart our early course at Alberto-Culver. I came up with a concept I called "65 percent available" to describe my own personal approach to pricing and cost management. The term was meant to remind Bernice and me that every dollar we took in should bring with it sixty-five cents to be allocated to advertising, promotion, and profit. The other thirty-five cents covered our production and shipping costs and our overhead. We worked to keep extremely tight control on manufacturing costs; really, once we got going, it was almost down to zilch. We watched every penny closely. We felt we had to do so or risk losing in the marketplace. As I said, we didn't want the Alberto VO5 product to be dismissed as a "value" product—that is, an item normally found in a discount store—but, at the same time, we didn't want to price it out of reach of first-time users.

One of the other initiatives I undertook, which I was later told was an unusual step for a privately held company in those days, was to form a board of directors to oversee the management and direction of our efforts. I appointed Stone and Arrington to the board, along with my own personal attorney, and determined to add good and well-informed people to it as they crossed my path. In this way, I thought, we'd grow our knowledge base exponentially and build a seamless connection between big-picture management and small-strokes operations.

Whatever we did, we saw the positive results almost immediately. Sales of Alberto VO5 tripled in our first full year of operations, and they tripled again the following year, which meant that we did one million dollars in business at the close of 1956. And as the money came in and we studied the numbers, Bernice and I took great personal satisfaction that we were on to something, something big, something that could sustain us for the rest of our working lives, and something that we could pass down to our children.

Indeed, if we played it right and caught a few breaks early on, we both knew this Alberto-Culver enterprise could grow into something far bigger than either one of us had dared to imagine.

# 5

## Business as Usual

THOSE EXCITING FIRST MONTHS AT ALBERTO-CULVER RAN INTO EACH other like no time at all, and one of the most enjoyable aspects of the new business was the chance it gave me to work alongside my wonderful wife, Bernice. Ours was truly a full-fledged partnership, personally and professionally. I'll detail our bustling family life a bit later on in this book, but, for now, let me set it down for the record that Bernice was undoubtedly my key partner in growing the company. Indeed, she's been my key partner in all things, which I also want to establish for posterity, but I wish to focus here on the professional aspects of my life. As treasurer and secretary, Bernice had her hands in every part of the business, with an incredible attention to detail and overview. As my best friend and confidant, she was my "eyes and ears" on company matters; what I couldn't see or hear for myself, Bernice picked up on as a matter of course and reported back to me. As the company grew—and it grew quickly!—our working relationship essentially allowed me to be in two places at one time. Bernice monitored goings-on in one area, while I toiled in another.

As a matter of not-always-so-practical course, I recommend this type of setup wholeheartedly to anyone starting out in business. In fact, I'm quick to advise people just starting out in business to marry a whippersnapper like Bernice to cover their backs

*Leonard and
Bernice Lavin, late
1950s or early 1960s*

and make them look good. (I'll tell you, it's better than any M.B.A.
degree.) What was especially gratifying, early on, was the way Bernice and I were the first to arrive at the office each morning and
the last to close up shop each night. Most days, anyway, that was
how it went when we weren't traveling, busy with a school event
for the children, or doing something of a personal nature. I don't
mean to sound hokey about it, but we looked to run the company
like a real mom and pop operation.

Of course, as the company got bigger, that became harder and
harder to do, but, in the beginning, we made it a point to have a
handle on everything. I felt we could never be too big for Bernice
and me to worry over the small, day-to-day details. I don't think
our employees minded our total involvement because we were

fairly up front about it—and pretty nice about it, too, if I can offer my subjective view. The legendary baseball player Leo Durocher, who later managed the beloved Chicago Cubs, famously declared that nice guys finish last. I didn't agree with him; Bernice and I felt strongly that we would do well to create a winning, comfortable, friendly environment for our company. We may have been demanding, but we never were difficult; we may have been perfectionists, but we were also the first to allow that we weren't perfect ourselves. We made many of our significant early hires in consultation with each other, and we constantly made an effort to treat our employees like family. Actually, to call this last an *effort* is perhaps overstating things a bit because it was no effort at all. There was a genuine family business facet to our affairs, and, once you were in the Alberto-Culver fold, you really were a part of the family. Naturally, families being what they are, the extended Alberto-Culver clan didn't always get along or agree on every matter, but we all treated each other decently and with a degree of kindness and caring not found in most businesses.

As a conscious management style, this can be a good thing or a bad thing, depending on your approach. In our experience, it ran mostly to the good, although there were times when friendships and relationships clouded my better business judgement. Over the years, I've invariably made some decisions I've come to regret, particularly in areas of personnel, and these were often made doubly hard to swallow for the friendships that usually formed in each case. In the beginning, that was the culture Bernice and I were determined to instill in the business, one of caring and familiarity, and, for the most part, it worked to our tremendous advantage. Comb through our ranks as our company approaches its fiftieth year, and you'll see dozens of essential, top-level people who've climbed our internal corporate ladder, working with us for their entire careers and leaving the Alberto-Culver Corporation far richer for their having joined us in the first place. This, too, has been a great, good thing.

*A meeting of the original Alberto-Culver board of directors, 1962*

In that first year, though, our numbers were still small. We were not yet the big business we soon became. We had our sales force, naturally, and our board of directors, and we gradually added layers of management in areas like marketing. We also added support personnel in purchasing, production, legal, and so on, but I was never the sort of boss who could delegate authority completely to one of my staff. Or, I should say, it took me a while to learn how to do so, and a while longer to do so regularly. I had to know everything that was going on, down to the finest point, and this, I feel, was one of my great strengths as a leader and strategist, and also one of my great weaknesses. Obviously, if you hire the right people, they can steer the ship while you chart the course; it's one thing to be hands-on, and quite another to be all-hands-on-deck, to milk the sea-faring metaphor for all it's worth. In my case, I occasionally erred on the side of control. But that was, and remains, my nature, so I've had to work with the tools I'd been given, right?

During our second year of business, two new-product initiatives came into play that nicely illustrated the positives and negatives to this type of approach. One of these new products was a hit, and the other, quite frankly, was a miss. Rinse Away, an anti-dandruff product, became a big success for Alberto-Culver—a perennial winner. It grew directly from my over-involvement in sales and new product development and placement. See, we had good salespeople in place to cover all of the chains and professional outlets, and part of their jobs was to be on the lookout for other products we perhaps could add to our line. Those were our marching orders to *all* Alberto-Culver employees: be ever on the lookout for new opportunities. Remember, I always made a point of asking our buyers if there was anything interesting or innovative that we might want to take a look at. It was this painstaking approach that took me to Alberto VO5 in the first place, so the business plan was to keep open to every possibility that came our way. The trouble was, I just wasn't patient enough for them to report back with the perfect opportunity, so when a follow-up item didn't come over the transom right away, I went looking. We had our guys out there, ostensibly doing the same thing, but, for some reason, my instincts took me to Pasadena, California. I'd heard about this Rinse Away product from a number of key West Coast contacts, and I felt that we could do well with it. There was really no other item like it marketed in any kind of national way, and I felt certain that it would click with consumers, so I paid a visit to the manufacturer. Here again, it was a product without any real muscle behind it sold mostly to the regional professional market.

As it happened, I was in Hawaii, opening up our warehouse and factory operations there, when I was tipped to Rinse Away. I was able to get an appointment with the manufacturer en route to Chicago. In those days, of course, they didn't have jet service like they do today, and there was no direct flight from Hawaii to Chicago anyway. I took advantage of the stop in Los Angeles to drive out to Pasadena to see if there was anything to this anti-dandruff product. Happily, there was; I made an aggressive offer for the product, and, by the time I stepped back on the plane for Chicago, I had in place a good faith deal to buy the item. I put my people to work on it right away. We looked to build it up the same way we'd done with the Alberto VO5 brand: with television advertising when we could afford it, repackaging, repositioning, and a shift in focus to the consumer market instead of to the professional market. Show me a proven formula for success, and I'll grab it every time.

I made one of my most significant early hires during this period by reaching out to an advertising executive named Jeff Wade, who inherited an agency from his father. Wade was doing attention-getting work for Alka-Seltzer. I thought that experience would be helpful to us because Alka-Seltzer was a consumer product that relied on aggressive television advertising. Wade and his team had the tools in place to get us noticed. What also worked in our favor was the fact that Alka-Seltzer was Wade's only other client, which meant that he had a good deal of time to devote to our effort. As it turned out, Wade was instrumental in our successful relaunch of the Rinse Away product, which quickly emerged as a market leader, and also in the fine-tuning of our Alberto VO5 advertising. It was through our association with Wade that I made the acquaintance of Miles Laboratories president "Uncle" Charles Beasley (Miles, of course, was the lab behind Alka-Seltzer and several other well-known brands), and Mr. Beasley, in turn, put me onto a market research analyst named Ernst Dichter. Dichter ran a fairly prominent outfit called the Institute of Motivational Research, and I was persuaded to throw in with him in order to better position our brands with consumers. I must confess, I was a bit put off by the notion of setting aside my gut instincts in favor of carefully modulated market research, but Alka-Seltzer enjoyed enormous success following this guy's good advice, so I figured what the hell.

As I recall, Dichter's first fee was fifty thousand dollars, which is still an awful lot of money to spend on market research, but, back in 1956, the amount was positively sinful. Even so, we bit the bullet and went ahead with the arrangement. After all, this guy had some great successes advising not only Alka-Seltzer, but also the big American automobile companies and other well-known brands, such as Campbell's Soup. The institute's directive was to help us determine why people used Alberto VO5 hairdressing. We would use the findings to inform our advertising effort going forward. Dichter conducted all kinds of focus groups and tests and, before long, came back with his report. He told us that the "key words" that customers responded to in relation to our product were "dull," "dry," and "hard to manage," which, of course, were used to describe the various types of hair that could benefit from our hairdressing. This was important information because it helped Jeff Wade focus our advertising. Alberto VO5 gave hair sheen, it gave it moisture, and it made hair more manageable. These words and phrases became the focus of our advertising, and we saw a direct bump in sales once the new campaign kicked in. By the end of 1958, just to give you some barometer of the success we had with VO5 and the Rinse Away product, company-wide sales topped five million dollars, representing huge, off-the-chart growth from our baseline volume of one hundred thousand dollars just four years earlier.

I was particularly intrigued by some of Dichter's findings and his no-nonsense approach to marketing. "Leonard," he told me, in making his report, "most women don't believe you when you show them this beautiful high-fashion model on television with a beautiful hair-do, and you tell them they can achieve the same look with your product. They don't feel they're in the same league. What they want to hear is that you have an item that will help them look better, something they can relate to. They don't want to look like fashion models, but they want to look better, and they want the convenience your products offer."

It really was eye-opening because up until that time, most of our television and print advertising used high-fashion models to prove our point, and now I was hearing from Ernst Dichter that this was possibly overkill. Not only was it more than we needed to make our sale, it was possibly off-putting to the average American woman, and so we needed to do some retooling in our approach. Jeff Wade, to his credit, was quick to embrace Dichter's recommendations, and soon all of our advertising carried more of an "average" person feel. We still marketed our products to women, but felt strongly that VO5 and Rinse Away held appeal to men as well, and Dichter's research reinforced this too.

Most of our early television advertising was placed on daytime programs, which, in those days, meant soap operas and game shows. *The Price Is Right* and *Guiding Light* were some of our biggest buys in the beginning. Most of the soap operas were sponsored by Procter and Gamble, which soon emerged as our big-footed competitor in the hair-care, personal hygiene, and cosmetics arena, so those shows were not available to us. Even today, Procter and Gamble controls much of the soap opera market; it owns several of the most popular programs outright. But there were several sponsorships open to us then, and we seized the ones that made sense for our products and our growing advertising budget.

Now, on to another product launch that was something less than successful. Actually, it was an out-and-out failure, and I have only myself to blame. We developed a product called Command for Men, which was essentially another hairdressing and styling product on the order of Alberto VO5, with the main difference that it was marketed directly to men. It had a slightly different fragrance than our flagship product, but I pushed ahead on the launch of this item, even though our research showed that perhaps there was no real market need. Alberto VO5, in our first two years of sales, enjoyed fantastic success among men. We didn't market the product to men, as I've written, and they didn't necessarily buy the stuff themselves, but they nevertheless used it in big numbers. Here, I thought that we could highlight that success with the specific packaging and placement of a new brand. It would work in the same way to achieve the same result, but I thought that we could distinguish the brands and create new sales, rather than merely siphoning off the sales of VO5 to men and placing them in the Command column.

Regrettably, neither outcome greeted us upon our product launch. The Command item was so-so with consumers. I realized later that I should have listened to the good people Bernice and I put in place, who all along indicated that there was no real hole in our market for such an item. Not only that, but the failure also reinforced for us that one of the principal reasons for VO5's early success was the professional endorsement behind it. With Alberto VO5, we inherited a brand that was built from the ground up with positive word-of-mouth from beauticians, hairstylists, and salon owners. We continued to use that line of attack in our initial advertising after I bought the company; we emphasized the professional endorsement of the item. With Command, however, we developed the thing from scratch, and there was no professional endorsement of which to speak. It was a good product, don't get me wrong, but we were unable to offer the customer a compelling reason to try it, and so it never paid off for the money invested.

With all of the stops and starts to this point in my career, this stalled product launch marked my first real professional failure, but I wouldn't let it trouble me. I was savvy enough to know that even our best instincts are sometimes off and that every effort can't possibly find its mark. You win some and you lose some, in life as in business, and I wasn't the sort to let myself be defined by the one any more than I would be marked by the other.

The key to our future success, I knew, would come from learning from our mistakes and making certain not to repeat them.

With our accelerating growth in sales came our related growth in manpower. Our production facilities needed to expand to keep pace with demand, and we needed to bolster our senior management team and support staff, as well. What this meant, in practical terms, was that we would soon outgrow Alberto-Culver's initial office and factory space at 251 East Grand Avenue in downtown Chicago. We had an entire floor in a big manufacturing building, and when we signed the lease, I felt it could accommodate our needs for a good long while, but I hadn't anticipated such rapid expansion. We had about one-third of the floor devoted to office space and two-thirds devoted to manufacturing, but it wasn't nearly enough to suit us for the foreseeable future, so I started shopping around for new headquarters.

In the early sixties, there were a number of princely office buildings sprouting in the downtown Chicago area. We could have had our pick of prime commercial real estate, but, as I studied each opportunity, I realized that any situation that seemed right for us in the near future would undoubtedly be too small for us before too long. It made no sense to take significantly more space than we needed at just that moment, but, at the same time, it made no sense to design a new plant that we soon would outgrow. Plus, as a tenant, I was forever subjected to the shifts in the real estate market, so I decided to buy an entire building at 4201 West Grand Avenue. It yielded about forty thousand square feet of space. It sounds like a lot of room, I know, but we filled it up pretty quickly, and I remember surveying the space one afternoon shortly before we took occupancy and marveling to myself how far we'd come in such a short stretch of time, how quickly we'd grown. Really, it was a wondrous thing to think back to my first visit to Alberto-Culver "headquarters" in Los Angeles: I stood over an old oil drum filled with Alberto VO5, learned how to mix the formula, and bet five hundred thousand dollars of my partners' money that we could make a nice run with this product. And here, in just a few short years, we flourished to the point that we now needed forty thousand square feet of our own space. I allowed myself a small smile of satisfaction. With sales in excess of five million dollars, we needed production facilities and executive offices to match, so I became a real estate mogul as well.

One of our first orders of business in our new headquarters was to make the most intelligent use of this expanded space to keep our production line busy and so forth. We did this to a degree as a matter of course because of the advancing popularity of our hairdressing and antidandruff products, but I once again turned my attention to acquisition to expand our line. If it was easy or predictable to develop products from scratch, we'd all be rich, so I knew I had to look for proven lines and products that were possibly floundering due to poor management or vision. If, as occasionally happened, we managed to pioneer a new product, then that would be wonderful, but we needed to pursue both methods of growth to remain competitive.

I was tipped to a company called Godefroy in St. Louis, which manufactured an interesting (albeit under-performing) line of professional hair-coloring products under the name Tresemmé. We wanted to introduce the product into the retail markets, and, once again, we looked to television to get the word out. We created a beautiful commercial with extremely high production values, but, for some reason, we couldn't move the item. This was hot on the heels of our Command disappointment, so when sales of Tresemmé continued to flatline, I became alarmed. It was okay, I realized, to misjudge the market once, or even from time to time, but to misjudge it back-to-back left me feeling off my game. Here we went out and bought an entire building to house our growing concern, and our two most recent product launches were going bust. Whatever confidence I had going into this phase of our development was just about shot—until it dawned on me that I needed to look at the reason the Tresemmé line did not catch on. With Command, the reason was clear: there was nothing to distinguish the upstart product from the bellwether brand. Whatever Command could have done for the consumer, Alberto VO5 had been doing better, longer, more reliably, more prominently, and with the seal of approval from the professional salon community. The Tresemmé failure was another story. Here we had a very good product in a burgeoning market backed by professional endorsements. There was no reason for a line like this *not* to catch on, provided we did our jobs in marketing, packaging, advertising, and promotion.

The only conclusion I could reach was that we had dropped the ball in one of these areas, and I was determined to discover which one. And why. The failure, I gradually realized, was in the positioning of the item. The blame, I allowed, had to fall to me. After all, if you're going to take credit for the various successes that find your business along the way, you also must claim responsibility for the turns that don't quite work out as planned.

The television commercials, for all their glitz and high-production, were off target, and it was from this point forward that we made test commercials for each and every one of our advertising spots. We retained an advertising visionary named Horace Schwerin to conduct the testing. Schwerin had this whole system devised that was really a kind of genius, in its own manner, for the way he dissected a spot, took the consumer's pulse, and gauged the results. He really had a very sophisticated, systematic approach to measuring the effectiveness of a single commercial or an entire campaign. Over time, his work proved to be an invaluable marketing tool. It got so that we spent more money on testing the commercials than we spent on actually producing them, and once we retooled the Tresemmé line, we began to see an almost immediate bump in sales. The mistake was not using Horace Schwerin right out of the gate, and this gaffe was made doubly glaring because we already had experience with him through the Alka-Seltzer products. His reputation was such that he was a known commodity in the field and a recognized asset. Indeed, his results spoke volumes about what we did right and wrong, in each case, and yet we'd allowed ourselves to be seduced by a gorgeous television spot, never realizing that a gorgeous spot is not necessarily an effective spot.

This hard lesson roughly coincided with the difficult decision to replace our advertising guru, Jeff Wade, who, by now, had become a good friend. This wasn't done in a finger-pointing way, and I wasn't the sort of executive to go calling for heads or hides when things didn't go our direction. If there was to be any finger-pointing on this or any other failing, it would have to be aimed at me; as president and chief executive, I was the person ultimately responsible. I don't mean this in a general, management-style sense, but in a very specific, practical sense. I was so intimately involved in every aspect of our business that if something did not work, I blamed myself. There was no one else to call to task. Jeff Wade was by no means the scapegoat in our stalled launch of new products, but the experience did point out a few gaps in our approach that needed to be filled, so I moved to fill them. I began to look at the folks at Procter and Gamble as our giant rival because even though we were still pipsqueaks compared to them, our biggest selling lines were so successful that they were, as often as not, number one in their product categories. Nevertheless, I started to pay careful attention to Procter and Gamble's packaging, their advertising, and their other maneuverings in markets where we went head-to-head. I'd been quite impressed lately with some of their television commercials. Really, Procter and Gamble did a lot of things well for such a big company, and advertising was one of them. The company's commercials were quite effective.

I asked around and learned that a New York outfit called Compton Advertising was responsible for much of Procter and Gamble's advertising, so I put a call in to the head of the agency, Bart Cummings. I did this on the theory that if you've got a target in mind, there's no profit in shooting for the outer circles; it only pays to aim for the bull's-eye.

Now, we may have been pipsqueaks compared to Procter and Gamble, but our advertising budget represented a rather sizeable account to an agency. We weren't a charity case, by any stretch. We were significant players, beginning in the late 1950s, as our sales really began to take off, and a guy like Bart Cummings was happy to take a call from a guy like me. He was even happy to come out to Chicago to pitch for our business. We looked at a few other agencies during this time, of course, but I was fairly impressed with Cummings and his Compton team—not least because of his association with Procter and Gamble. What concerned me, however, was the thought of doing business long distance with a New York agency. I knew this sort of thing was done all the time—really, it was standard practice—but I didn't feel that it was right for Alberto-Culver. The company was at a point in its growth where we were adding new products and moving in new directions. We already had such a considerable advertising budget and commercial production schedule that I wanted our agency people to be close at hand, so I decided to make Cummings a pitch of my own.

"Bart," I told him, "I'd like to go with your agency, but I want to pick your top people and bring them out here."

"What do you mean, Leonard?" he asked, quite reasonably. As far as I knew, the custom in the industry was for the client to go to the agency and not the other way around.

"I mean, I want you to establish an office in Chicago," I explained. "Let me go back to New York with you and put together a team."

He thought this over for a bit and realized that it could be a very lucrative situation for his company because, of course, once he opened an office in Chicago, he was free to solicit other business there as well. Our fees would essentially bankroll Compton Advertising's satellite office, and all other monies that came in on top of ours would be gravy.

So I went to New York and interviewed all of Compton's best people. Account managers, research directors, creative types—all down the line. Obviously, not everyone was interested in relocating to Chicago, but there were enough talented young people who were willing to move to make my position viable. We assembled a top team and began a very profitable association for both concerns. On our end, we worked with some of the most talented, forward-thinking people in the advertising community; on Compton's, they opened up a new market with very little risk. Plus, as the years went on, we proved to be a very deep-pocketed client. As our sales soared—we crossed the fifty million dollar threshold in 1960—our advertising budget followed. At one point fairly early on in our history, I realized that we spent tens of millions of dollars each year on television advertising alone. These numbers would have been unthinkable to me just a few years earlier, but here they were—and there was no denying that it was worth every penny.

It was a far cry from those very first television advertising buys when Bernice and I combed our books each week to squeeze what was left into whatever commercial time we could afford. We still stretched our advertising budget as far as it would go, but the stakes were much higher.

And, as the stakes grew, so did we. Soon enough, our new offices on West Grand Avenue weren't big enough to hold us because we'd expanded so quickly. This time, I looked to build a building instead of buying one. I looked in a part of town where land was reasonably affordable and where opportunity beckoned. The city fathers were opening up a new airport closer to midtown, and I felt it would be worthwhile to inch a bit closer to the site. Up until this time, the only Chicago-area airport was Midway, but O'Hare would be a lot more convenient to the downtown area.

I came across a parcel of land out in Melrose Park, a Chicago suburb that would put us in close proximity to O'Hare, and it was very attractively priced. One of the reasons the land was so affordable was that a train line passed right through it. Most businesses weren't interested in building right alongside someone else's train tracks, particularly when those tracks bisected the available property, but I did not let this fact deter me from a good prospect, so I went out to the area and timed the trains. It made no sense to debate this dilemma in the abstract when there was good, hard evidence to be collected, so I made the effort to do so. For some reason, I couldn't get a train schedule. It was a small freight line running across the property, so I prepared to park myself there for a while until a train came through. Well, it might have been a fool's errand because the trains didn't come through more than once each week, but I would have been a fool to pass up such cheap land. Really, other than the small inconvenience of the railroad tracks, it was prime real estate that needed a buyer. The property was owned by a wealthy Chicago family, which owned the Armour meat packing company, as I recall; the owners were having a devil of a time getting rid of it. Folks just couldn't seem to get past these tracks, but I figured it wouldn't be much of a nuisance to have a train pass through once or twice each week. The tracks were situated in such a way that they really didn't interfere with any of the construction we planned to do, so I went ahead and pursued the property.

If memory serves, we bought the land for approximately fifty cents per square foot—a real steal if you discounted the railroad tracks, which I chose to do. I hired an architect, who designed a state-of-the-art, one-hundred-thousand-square-foot facility, and, forty years later, we still haven't outgrown the place. Actually, that is not entirely accurate: we quickly outgrew the initial facility and added on to it over the years. We've expanded the complex to approximately eight hundred thousand square feet, but we're still at the same address, and that counts for something.

What also counts, I'm happy to report, is that the financial community began to notice our efforts. I hate to resort to such an easy children's book reference, but since we were now situated alongside a stretch of railroad tracks, and since trains had become a weekly fact of our existence, it was not out of place to start thinking of our company as the little engine that could. That story was always a favorite in our household for the way it championed the little guy. The rallying cry from the story—"I think I can, I think I can, I think I can . . ."—easily could have been our watchwords at Alberto-Culver. After all, we were the consummate start-up, going head-to-head with some of the giants of corporate America, and chugging along and making good progress just the same.

Apparently, you didn't need to be one of the giants to attract the attention of Wall Street investors, even in the early 1960s.

There was a period in there, roughly coinciding with some of our more prominent secondary product launches, where the thing to do in the financial and investment banking communities was discover unsung companies like ours and take them public. In many ways, the frenzy was similar to what we all saw recently, at the close of the 1990s, with the rush to cash in with all the dot-coms and high-tech companies. Back then, I always was fearful of the result that ultimately found many of these hasty initial public offerings. Moreover, I never wanted to be confined by the constraints placed on public companies; we'd enjoyed tremendous success as a private concern to this point—and, relatedly, tremendous freedom—and I saw no reason to upset the apple cart.

Our board of directors, however, felt a public offering was a good path to consider, so I encouraged the conversation. We'd been approached by a number of financial types during our short history, but lately we'd been pursued by two groups of investment bankers who talked an impressive game: Virgil Sherill with Shields and Co. and Lehman Brothers. Bobby Lehman, the head of Lehman Brothers, in particular, showed himself to be a sound and savvy business mind. We lunched together whenever I was in New York, and, early in 1961, he convinced me to take Alberto-Culver public.

"Leonard," he used to say. "There's a lot of money to be made."

I never was opposed to making a lot of money, but I was concerned that there would be strings attached. Understand, we weren't out to raise capital, as is often the case when a company goes public. We were able to finance almost all of our growth and acquisitions through cash flow. Other than a few modest loans here and there, we carried virtually no debt, which was highly unusual for a company of our size. But, even though we didn't *need* the money, it was difficult—and, perhaps, impractical—to look away from the opportunity.

The plan, as laid out by Sherill and Lehman Brothers, was to list our company on the over-the-counter exchange, and Bobby

Lehman took me around to various brokerage houses and financial institutions on what he called a "road show". A road show, for those of you who have never had the pleasure of being on either end of the ordeal, is essentially a dog-and-pony show. The investment bankers trot out their company executives, who are made to sing the praises of their various businesses and jump through enough hoops to give the impression that a stake in our company was a sound investment. In this respect, I suppose, these motions had as much to do with beauty pageantry as they did with commerce, but who was I to question such established practice? I remember fielding questions like, "How are you going to compete with Procter?" Or, "How are you going to compete with Johnson and Johnson?" And my answer was always the same: "We've competed with them so far."

As it happened, we went public in 1961 with an offering price of ten dollars per share. This number was determined by the investment bankers and based on what they felt was the relative worth of our company set against an acceptable multiple of our projected earnings. Somewhere in there they also factored in a price point that would be acceptable to the marketplace. I didn't think to question their methods. Actually, let me correct that last statement because, as I've indicated, I questioned everything relating to the prospects of our company, right down to the last nickel and dime. So, yes, I did question Bobby Lehman when he came to me with his price. I looked over the numbers with him and listened to his reasoning. What I didn't question was his expertise. This was his business, and, presumably, he knew his business like I knew mine; once I threw in with him, I was prepared to follow his lead. What did I know about establishing an offering price for our company? I could tell you what our book value was; I could look at our sales history; I could detail some of the new products in our development pipeline and project our growth. But the good people at Sherill and Lehman Brothers knew what the market would bear and what made sense, so we went out at ten dollars per share and that was that.

I should mention here that we carved out a still small but potentially thriving piece of our business from the public offering. Our international business, which at that early stage was nothing like it became in later years, was kept out of our initial prospectus on the theory that in this one area, at least, we needed to be aggressive and unencumbered going forward. Plus, it was determined that our domestic business was more than enough to sustain a healthy, attractive public offering, so it made no sense to throw the component parts into the mix if they didn't impact our offering price. (As it happened, however, the international business was rolled into the parent company two or three years later.)

Well, the offering was oversubscribed. There were more people wanting to buy shares of our young company than we had blocks of shares to offer. Realize, we only made a small percentage of company stock available to the public, wanting to keep the company a closely held concern going forward. But, by the end of the first few days, our stock sold for twenty-two dollars per share in over-the-counter trading. Almost overnight, the market value of our company more than doubled. Our net worth, on paper at least, soared. Of course, such an impressive run right out of the gate wasn't at all unusual during the bull market the country recently experienced, but back then, the initial public offerings (IPOs) didn't run up in price like that in such rapid fashion. I took it to mean that perhaps we underestimated the public's appetite for a sound, steady business like ours, or that we had been a shade conservative in assessing our potential for growth.

Whatever the reason, I was happy that investors had been so taken with our little company. I wasn't so happy about some of the constraints that were placed on our business now that we had a responsibility to our shareholders. It's one thing to be beholden to your bottom line, your board of directors, or your private investors. It's quite another to be accountable to individuals all across the country and to be concerned about posting earnings increases every quarter, dividend increases, and things of that nature. There have been times over the years when I've felt that the company could have grown five times bigger if I was free to take certain risks. I don't mean to suggest that I was ever the sort to gamble with company funds; in fact, I took great pride in being somewhat fiscally conservative. Before taking the company public, I never looked to finance a deal we couldn't otherwise afford; if I couldn't pay for a struggling business or product out of receivables, I usually let the opportunity pass. So, clearly, I wasn't playing fast and loose with the company checkbook, but the reality is that you're rendered especially conservative once you've got shareholders to whom you must report. And, frankly, there were certain rolls of the dice I couldn't even consider as a publicly held concern.

Still, it was a wondrous, affirming thing to open the financial papers each morning and see our name listed right there alongside these other giants of corporate America. To be able to chart our growth in such a public way. To know that from our meager initial stake, and inherited first year sales of just one hundred thousand dollars, we were now a thriving, growing concern, to the point where people wanted to own a piece of our business.

⁂

Let me share another remarkable turn before closing this chapter in our development. Regrettably, it closed my association with Bart Cummings of Compton Advertising. We certainly had nothing but high praise for his efforts and would have loved to continue our association with his company, but we were cunningly big-footed out of the relationship.

Not long after our initial public offering, we introduced a new product that might have been something of a revolution in first aid. We developed a medicated bandage that wasn't really a bandage at all, but a spray. It was, I felt certain, a major breakthrough. The spray was applied to the injured area, then it dried to form a protective coating. It acted essentially like a bandage, and, at the same time, treated the cut or scrape with the appropriate medications. It was one of our first forays into non-hair products, and we were all terribly excited about the item and its applications. We called it Safe Guard and introduced it into the marketplace with high expectations.

We prepared an interesting series of commercials to launch the product, and as they began to air, I took a call from Bart Cummings. He wanted to come in and talk to me, and from the sound of his voice, it seemed like something was troubling him. He cut right to it when he came to see me. "Leonard," he said, "I've been called in by Procter. They told me if I wanted to keep their business, I can no longer handle your advertising."

I was dumbfounded. Bart's people at Compton did a wonderful job promoting our products. He came up with a fairly unique style of advertising that we used to call "torture test" campaigns: we put our hairspray products to some sort of extreme test and demonstrated how they performed under extraordinary conditions. Frequently, we tested our products alongside less successful products of our unnamed competitors. The most famous of such commercials were not created for one of our products, but most people remember the successful series of Timex ads. In them, wristwatches were submitted to all kinds of rough treatment and found to be still ticking. We had some memorable spots of our own, however, most notably a series we produced at the famous blowhole on Oahu, where we positioned women in such a way that their hair was hit with great force by the water and yet they still looked great afterward. So, clearly, I wasn't happy to hear of Bart's dilemma. I hated to lose good people for no good reason, and I felt it was possible for friendly competitors to share an independent asset like Compton Advertising without concern on either side. It seemed to me to be a cheap shot on Procter's part, a petty maneuver, to ask Bart to choose sides.

"What do you want to do?" I asked Bart.

"I don't think I have any choice," he said. "Procter's my biggest client. I need their business."

Of course, I understood. I hated it, but I understood, and I wished Bart Cummings and his people well.

But there was something else going on at Procter, which was related to our Safe Guard product. Undoubtedly, this led to the "showdown" with Compton. Incidentally, the product didn't appear to be the hit we all hoped it would be. It was selling, but I wasn't getting the type of return I was used to seeing on the hair-care items. My thinking was to milk the product and move on to the next thing. To "milk" a product meant to continue to sell it and fulfill orders, but to suspend all advertising and other active means of promotion. We'd produce it and ship it, but we wouldn't advertise it in any way, and eventually demand for the item would simply disappear and we would shut down production. So, that's where we were on Safe Guard at approximately the time we were winding down our relationship with Bart Cummings. It was during this period that I received a strange telephone call from a man who introduced himself as a Procter and Gamble attorney. We didn't have a legal department at that time, so I took the call myself.

"Mr. Lavin," he announced, "you're infringing on one of our trademarks."

Without even knowing what he was talking about, I knew this fellow was off base. We had some top-notch trademark and patent attorneys working with us at the time, and I knew we were covered in this area, whatever this man's claim happened to be. "What are you talking about?" I asked.

"Your Safe Guard bandages," he said. "We're developing a product by that name, and we've secured the necessary trademark."

"Nonsense," I said. "We registered the name before we took it to market. You better go and recheck your paperwork."

But this man was adamant about it, so I put a call in to the outside law firm handling such matters to get to the bottom of the situation. Our attorneys told me, in no uncertain terms, that we were indeed covered on this, and that the name was registered to us for use in markets all around the world. He advised me to let the matter slide, and so I did. Apparently, Procter and Gamble was looking to launch a soap called Safeguard, with which I believe they still do very well, and they felt that we were sitting on a product name that was rightfully theirs.

About a week later, the Procter attorney phoned me again. "Mr. Lavin," he began, "we would like you to cease and desist from the use of this name."

I didn't much like it when people told me to cease and desist from anything, particularly a thing that I had every legal right to do, but I wasn't looking to pick an argument with this man. I even thought about coming clean and telling him we were planning to milk the item. Actually, I came close to doing just that. I said, "Look, I don't want to fight with Procter and Gamble. We don't have the resources. I'm not so sure we're continuing with that line anyway, so if you just wait a while the problem will go away."

If ever there was a white flag being raised in surrender to a corporate giant, this was apparently it, but the attorney would not be put off. In fact, he was very aggressive about it, almost belligerent. I got off the phone thinking that if he only had been pleasant, I might have told him the entire story, how we were looking to kill the line anyway, and everyone would have been happy.

Once again, on the advice of our attorneys, I decided to ignore the demand, and we went about our business. After a few days, I received a registered legal notice that Procter and Gamble was taking us to federal court to have the matter settled. I was incensed. I was bothered by the nuisance this matter quickly became and infuriated at being pitted against the big boys in such a public way. I called our patent attorneys and told them that I wanted to hit back. "What can we do?" I wondered to an attorney, and he had me walk him through the entire Safe Guard story, including the piece about Bart Cummings being strong-armed into dropping our business. At this, the attorney concluded that we had a hell of an antitrust case against Procter, so I told him to file a counter claim—also in federal court. I knew we were on firm ground on this matter, so I had no qualms about countering Procter and Gamble's aggressive legal position with one of our own.

The very next day, my secretary came into my office to tell me that Neil McElroy was on the phone. Neil McElroy, the chairman of the board at Procter and Gamble, had been secretary of defense under President Eisenhower. He was a big, top guy, with a big, top reputation, and he couldn't have been more cordial when I got on the phone with him. He suggested that we "friendly competitors" get together and talk, and I agreed to a lunch meeting in the Procter and Gamble boardroom. I asked if it was okay if I brought along my attorneys, and he said by all means, so I called my personal attorney and our trademark attorney and made arrangements for them to accompany me to Procter's headquarters in Cincinnati.

As we entered the company's offices, I realized just how big the moment was. I mean, Procter was positively huge compared to us. We were like an ant they could have stepped on. Everything about them was huge, and their offices were austere, imposing, and impressive as hell. We were made to wait by ourselves for a few moments in the boardroom, dwarfed by giant portraits of Mr. Procter and Mr. Gamble, and I remember thinking that maybe we were out of our league on this one. Maybe the old saw that you can't always get what you want didn't necessarily apply to corporate giants. But then I remembered that we were in the right, and that things would shake out in our favor. That's the way we're always taught, isn't it? That the good guys prevail. That might doesn't make right. That it doesn't take a judge to tell you what's fair. I allowed myself to think these things as I sat beneath the colossal gazes of Mr. Procter and Mr. Gamble, reassuring myself of our strong position.

Neil McElroy joined us soon enough, along with his team of lawyers and advisers—as I recall, we were outnumbered by a significant margin—and there were handshakes and introductions all around. Mr. McElroy began the meeting by announcing that he and his colleagues were "high church people," an expression I'd never heard before. but took to mean that they were ethical businessmen. (I'll resist the easy jokes about how the term is an oxymoron.) I didn't know what to say to an introduction such as this, so being a wiseacre at heart, I responded, "Well, Mr. McElroy, I'm a nice Jewish boy, but I think that still puts us on the same page."

This seemed to get things off on the right foot, and, before long, it was apparent that these guys wanted to reach some sort of settlement. They didn't want to drag either of these cases through the courts, even though they had the deep pockets to outlast us on both fronts. And so, we made a deal. Procter offered us a kind of "kill fee" to cease and desist from marketing our Safe Guard medicated bandage product and to drop our antitrust suit so that they could go forward with the launch of their Safeguard bathroom soap. I grabbed at their terms immediately, thinking that it was a fairly sweet deal for Alberto-Culver and a fairly foolish one for Procter and Gamble. After all, we planned to phase out the Safe Guard product anyway, and we indicated as much to them in prior exchanges. Once we had milked our inventory, we happily would have parted with the rights to the name for a whole lot less. But they were "high church people," and it wouldn't do to have their good company name dragged through the mud in an antitrust case, just as it wouldn't do to appear less than generous in reaching for a settlement. Naturally, once they made such an offer, we "nice Jewish boys" couldn't talk them down from it; we couldn't even try. After all, we now had the benefit of our shareholders to consider, and we couldn't look away from such a windfall on their behalf.

And so I contented myself with the knowledge that we bested the big boys in our first head-to-head clash. What was especially gratifying was the way we got something for nothing. Indeed, as time went on, I took special pleasure in taking them on in a variety of ways, as the opportunities arose. I saw another opening soon after the Safe Guard impasse, for example. It involved our new Alberto VO5 hairspray, the first crystal-clear hairspray, which quickly emerged as a market leader upon its introduction in 1961. During the small talk surrounding the Safe Guard negotiations with McElroy and his people, McElroy let slip that Procter planned to introduce its own hairspray later that year after a successful run in several test markets.

I cautioned him against such a move. "I don't think you understand the hairspray business," I told him, boldly. "I think you're soap people. That's what you do, and you do it well." I always felt that it was a good, disarming practice to cloak a criticism inside a compliment.

McElroy thanked me for my unsolicited advice and said that the product was testing well and that they were making ready for a national launch. He was even kind enough to tell me when they were rolling out the product across the country. What he meant as mere small talk, I took as a competitive edge. I wasn't about to let these "high church people" beat us at our own game, so I went back to Chicago and redoubled our efforts to keep the Alberto VO5 hairspray out in front. I decided to offer 35 percent more hairspray in each can in time for Procter's launch of its own hairspray. That way, we could blunt the impact of their new product. What better way to short-circuit their sales than to give our stuff away for free?

We loudly advertised the bonus amount on each can and in our television spots. We also produced another wonderful series of "torture test" ads featuring pretty girls on surfboards putting their hair through the toughest possible paces. At the end of the day, the salt, waves, and sun still did not undo their curls. There were other, somewhat less pretty girls who donned other, somewhat less effective hairsprays, and their curls, of course, couldn't hold up to the rigors of the ocean. Our product was left looking like a winner.

I loved the spots for their simple effectiveness and for the way that they allowed us to beat Procter and Gamble at its own game. After all, the commercials were based on a model of advertising developed by Bart Cummings and Compton Advertising before they were pushed from our business. We simply put Cummings's proven technique to work for us.

Still, I knew we couldn't compete with Procter just on the fact that we had a better product backed by a better commercial. We had to blanket the airwaves in such a way that our advertising budget could approximate theirs. The only way to do it, I determined, was to take all of our advertising dollars away from every other Alberto-Culver product, for the time being, and concentrate the funds on this one effort. That's how it often goes in a small company—you have to focus on one product, even if it means less funding for another. This latest run-in confirmed that despite our huge sales and rapid growth, we were still a small company when measured against our competitors. And so our hairdressing, shampoos, and our antidandruff products all took a back seat while we established our hold on the hairspray market. In so doing, we were able to neutralize Procter's bigger advertising budgets.

The footnote to this story is that Procter rolled out its national campaign for its new hairspray on schedule. Readers old enough to remember them might recall the spots featuring Wanda the Witch, but, despite the memorable campaign, Procter never was able to put a real dent in our market share. Within eighteen months, Wanda went away; the company removed the product from shelves and abandoned it entirely.

The abiding lesson to this story is that it sometimes pays to take what the competition gives you, whether it's a multimillion dollar windfall for doing what it is you'd already planned to do or a pull-out-the-stops campaign to dull a rival product launch.

Once again to differ with Leo Durocher on this one point: nice guys do not *always* finish last, but socially correct businessmen too polite to seize advantage and opportunity often do.

# 6

## Family

I T'S A FUNNY THING, THE WAY WE WORK SO LONG AND HARD TO BUILD some kind of foundation for the people we love the most. At least that's what drives many of us in our careers, and it's a big part of what's driven me for so many years. There are other people, and I count myself among this group as well, for whom the thrill of competition and the constant, striving push to do better or to do more is the be-all in business. But in almost every case, it comes down to family. Wouldn't you agree? We do what we do to make our mark and make a difference, yes, but mostly we do it to provide for our children and our grandchildren so that they might feel free to make other, more personal choices with their own careers.

This presents one of the great cultural paradoxes of our time. The harder we work, the more we are pulled from our families, which, at bottom, was the very reason we worked so hard in the first place. With me, this paradox stood as one of the defining aspects of my life in business because once I realized that I couldn't be in two places at one time, I also realized that my wife and children would do just fine without me—this one time. Regrettably, this one time too often led into another "one time," and by the time I looked up, there were all kinds of wonderful, intimate family moments lost to my busy schedule. More than any other disappointment relating to my career, this one keeps me up nights.

*The Lavin family: Scott, Bernice, Carol, Leonard, and Karen*

In fact, with my endless travel schedule and too-long hours at the office, we might never have started our young family, were it not for some extra efforts and maneuverings on the part of my wife Bernice. When we decided we wanted to have children, I was never at home long enough to do anything about it, to put it delicately, and so Bernice had to meet me on the road or accompany me if we hoped to accomplish our goal. That she did, and that we were able to find the time to conceive our three beautiful children, is testimony both to my wife's boundless spirit and good cheer and to my great, good fortune to have convinced her to throw in with me in the first place.

No, I didn't always do right by my family when our children were young—I'll be the first to admit it. In fact, I almost always did wrong. Frankly, in building this business, I deprived myself and my family of one of the big pleasures of life—togetherness. I traveled constantly. I don't mean to offer excuses for the decisions

I made or the special moments I missed, but I've often wondered what drove me so hard and kept me away for long periods from Bernice and our wonderful children. I think it had to do with a kind of genetic overreaching for success. It's a hand-me-down from my parents' generation, I think, this abiding thirst to succeed and then to succeed some more, this feeling that I needed to do it all myself, and that there was always something else that needed to get done. Remember, I lived through the Depression and was in the service for four and a half years, and when I got out, I was determined to build a business and start a family. The two were connected, but they didn't always fit hand-in-hand, if you know what I mean. I came out as a real hard-charger, extremely strong-willed and duty-bound to succeed.

Of course, if you ask my daughters now, or if you ask Bernice, they'll say our family life was just fine, and the truth is I didn't destroy our family any more than any other father of my generation. Indeed, I didn't destroy it at all, but I didn't put it first. Despite my attentions often being elsewhere and despite *me* often being elsewhere as well, Bernice and I managed to instill in our children a very strong, committed sense of family. That doesn't make me feel any better about what I missed, but I suppose it's the truth. We spent our Christmas vacations together, usually a welcome two-week respite and refueling out in Phoenix, but, other than that, I was gone more often than not. Even over Christmas, I sometimes fielded phone calls or took meetings that easily could have waited until after the holiday. I literally traveled fifty weeks out of the year, especially in those early years. Typically, I came back on Thursday or Friday nights, recharged my batteries, picked up a fresh change of clothes, attended to matters at home, and, by Monday, I was off on another flight. It was the only way to expand the business, I felt at the time. Looking over my shoulder, I still feel the same way. That sense of urgency to service all of the accounts personally, to chase down every new product lead, and to troubleshoot every snafu directly was compounded by the inconvenient air travel of the period, compared to the ease and freedom of jet travel today. If I wasn't out of town, I was in various stages of coming or going.

Bernice, for her part, was at the office every day, but she also was involved intimately with the children. No housewife had a better handle on how things were with her kids, and no businesswoman had a better handle on how things were with her company; truly, she didn't stint on a single thing, at home or at the office. My beautiful, fantastic wife was a kind of superwoman in this way and a generation or so ahead of her time. We had help around the house, to be sure, and this was enormously liberating for Bernice in terms of her work schedule. Bernice was home most afternoons after school, and she usually managed to squeeze in something a little extra special for the children beyond their daily routines. She often took some of the other neighborhood children with our kids to Kiddy Land, some amusement park, or out for ice cream. I always laughed to myself at the incongruity of the picture: Bernice Lavin, highlighted by *Fortune* magazine as one of the top ten businesswomen in corporate America, giving the stay-at-home mothers a break by taking their kids along on an outing after she logged a full day at the office.

We always felt that you found the time to do what needed to be done, or you made the time. We couldn't both be at each and every birthday party, school play, game, or recital. Most of the time it was Bernice who was there, but, on occasion, I was able to attend. Sometimes, I made it at the last minute or at great cost, but I tried to keep my word with my children. After all, if your kids can't trust you and believe in you, how can you ever expect them to believe in themselves? And so, whatever bargains I made with my kids over the years, I was careful to keep up my end. One such occasion has lapsed into Lavin family lore, and I share it here for the record and for the simple fact that it's *still* a good story.

Carol, my middle child and eldest daughter, was turning sixteen, and, as you might imagine, the sweet sixteen birthday was anticipated as a very big deal. I don't mean to diminish the

*Leonard Lavin and daughter Carol as a teenager*

significance of such a milestone because it truly was a big deal, and, naturally, it loomed as a great importance to Carol. We planned a wonderful family celebration down at our family horse farm in Florida. I'll fill in the blanks about how we came to own the horse farm and such in chapter 8.

Well, Carol was forceful in reminding me that I had missed more of her birthday celebrations than not, dating as far back as she could remember, due to my constant traveling and workaholic ways. She insisted on my personal guarantee that I would be in attendance this time around. How could I refuse? And, more to the point, why would I want to refuse after she put it to me in just that way? Nothing was more important—at least, nothing that was then on my schedule. So I gave her my word that I would be there, and I meant to keep it, but circumstances nearly derailed me from my best intentions.

A few weeks before Carol's birthday, I was invited to a White House dinner. I no longer recall the specific occasion, but it was a gathering of Chicago-area businessmen. Moreover, it was the first White House dinner to which I ever was invited, and I thought it would be nice to attend. I'd been to the White House before, but never to such a formal function. The date of the dinner was the evening before Carol's birthday party, so I felt fairly confident that I could travel to Washington, D.C., enjoy the dinner, and still make it down to Florida in plenty of time, even considering the vagaries of air travel during that period.

So, off to the White House I went, where I was joined by about fifty other prominent Chicagoans and President Richard M. Nixon, along with several other dignitaries. Happily, I found myself seated next to the president. We had met each other over the years at various functions, but he gave no indication that he remembered me; in fact, one of those meetings was of a more personal nature—another story I'll get to before long—but we made reintroductions just the same. The big topic of the day was the value-added tax, with which the Nixon administration was grappling at the time. There were widely divergent opinions on the issue; some economists felt that the United States should install such a tax as a means of raising revenues, and others felt that it would handcuff our economy by inflating the prices of domestic goods. The value-added tax, which allowed the government to tax manufacturers at each step in the manufacturing process, thereby driving up tax revenues and consumer prices, was the order of the day in most of the industrialized world, except in the United States. To us at Alberto-Culver, the fact that we operated without the tax offered a tremendous competitive advantage when we did business abroad (and, increasingly, we did a tremendous amount of business abroad) because we were able to undersell our competitors substantially. At the time, however, there were various pressures from various interests to get the United States to join these other countries in the practice, and the Nixon administration seemed to be pursuing this course.

Naturally, I had my own opinion on the matter, and since I was seated next to the president, I figured I would take the opportunity to press my case. "It will kill the economy," I insisted, when I had his attention. For some reason, I used an analogy comparing the value-added tax to the pulling of four empty railroad cars, which you still had to move along at a profit even though you weren't actually moving anything in those cars.

I'll give President Nixon credit: he was an attentive listener. He seemed deeply engaged in our conversation and very much interested in my opinions. At one point, he turned to me and said, "Leonard, I'm impressed with your theories. I'd like you to join me in my office tomorrow morning at nine o'clock. Secretary of Commerce Stans will be there, and I want you to tell him your position."

I was stuck. There I was, jawing with the president of the United States, invited back to the Oval Office the next morning to pursue my agenda on an important issue, perhaps even to help set important policy, and yet there was that previous commitment to my daughter, Carol, that I hated to break. I felt I had no choice but to turn down the president's request. "Mr. President," I said, sheepishly, "I'm afraid I can't make it tomorrow."

"Why not?" he wondered.

So I told him the story. I told him how I traveled extensively. How it was Carol's sixteenth birthday. How I hated the way my busy schedule kept me from so many important family moments. How I had given her my personal guarantee, and so forth. "If I don't fly down to Florida tonight, I won't be able to celebrate with her tomorrow," I said. "If I go back on my word, she'll never trust me again."

At this, the president craned his neck so that he could signal one of the formally dressed Marine officers who stood watch over the proceedings. The Marines really lent an air of pomp and circumstance to the affair with the way they decorated the room. Upon the summons from his commanding officer, a young lieutenant approached our table and handed the president a formal piece of stationary and a pen. President Nixon took the pen and paper and began to write: "Dear Carol. Your father is the only man who ever turned down a request from the president of the United States. Happy Birthday. President Richard M. Nixon."

I raced home to Florida that evening with a story to tell and a priceless keepsake to present to Carol as a memento of the occasion. And the story didn't end there. Approximately ten years later, long after President Nixon resigned his office in disgrace and long after Carol began working alongside me at Alberto-Culver, we attended a birthday party for our old friend Clement Stone. In addition to being one of the initial backers of our enterprise and a long-time member of our board of directors, Stone was also a prominent contributor to Republican Party candidates and, thus, a lifelong friend of Richard and Pat Nixon. All of which goes to explain how it was that former President Nixon was also in attendance, and, in fact, the Nixons were to be seated at the same table as Bernice and I.

"Hello, Leonard," he said as he approached the table for the first time, his arm extended in greeting, "How are you?" And, before I could respond, he added, "And how's Carol?"

It struck me then, as it does here in the retelling, as the most remarkable way for a former president to begin an exchange. What also struck me was that the president remembered my name and my daughter's. Really, for all his flaws as a leader, and for all the mistakes that were made in his name, on his watch, the man had a phenomenal memory.

"Really, how's Carol?" he asked again after we began talking. Again, I was astonished at his genuine interest.

"She's fine," I said. "In fact, she's here. Would you like to meet her?"

He said he would be honored to meet her, and when I brought Carol over to make the introductions, he told her the story all over again, about how I had stepped out on a meeting in his office so that I could get home in time for her birthday party—as if she hadn't heard it or retold it a hundred times herself.

Let me tell you, we've gotten a lot of mileage out of that story in our circle, and I tell it here for the way it reflects the constant tug and pull between our personal and professional lives. Too often, I put my business ahead of my family, but when it counted, when it *really* counted, family came first.

Ours was a busy household from the very beginning. Our oldest child, Scott, was a real rough and tumble kid. He was all boy, if you understand what I mean by the expression. He was born on October 23, 1949, at a time in our business lives when Bernice and I were reluctant to take our hands off the company throttle. Somehow, we managed to continue our rapid growth at Alberto-Culver, while, at the same time, we nurtured the rapid growth of our bustling baby boy. I can't tell you how thrilled I was to be the father of such a magnificent son. In many ways, Scott and I were cut from the same cloth; we were both headstrong, purposeful, and we loved to laugh and assemble a wide array of great, good friends. But he never had any affinity for the business, and that was just fine with Bernice and me. He worked in the factory as a young man, and he helped out in the office as an even younger man, but he made it clear to us that his interests lay elsewhere. Good for him, I thought at the time. Let him find something that makes him happy. Actually, let me put a fine point on this for the record: Scott did express *some* interest in the business—specifically, the casting of the young models and actresses who were in our commercials. Goodness, if he could have made a living doing such as that, he would have been content—and quite successful too, I might add.

One time I was in Beverly Hills interviewing models for a TV shoot with our agency people, and Scott came down from school to visit. He arrived about 1:00 P.M. and sat in for the rest of the day. That night at dinner, as he was just plowing into his second steak, he looked up at me and said, "Dad, you've got it made and you don't even know it."

Scott went to school out in California at Redlands University, and, in many ways, he became a California kid despite his midwestern upbringing. He worked peripherally in the entertainment

*Bernice Lavin and
daughter Karen*

business as an agent, a manager, and, eventually, a producer. He
also produced a terrific son out of a marriage that did not work
out, which reinforced for all of us that we sometimes can find the
brightest silver linings in the darkest clouds. And for all his Beverly Hills–style approaches to life and work, Scott had some real
successes here and there, and he constantly looked for the next
opportunity. In this way, I suppose, he was like his father.

When our youngest daughter Karen was born on January 8,
1956, Bernice took the company books with her to the hospital
for her maternity stay. In those days, women were kept on the maternity ward for several days, sometimes as long as a week, and
she felt that was too long to be away from the office, so she took
the office with her. That's the kind of dedication she had, during
a time when it was rather unusual to see a woman in the top levels of management for a top company.

*Karen Lavin,*
*1983*

Karen is our blithe spirit. She's never expressed an interest in the family business, and we've never pressed it on her. It's funny how Bernice and I dipped into the same gene pool three times and came up with three entirely different children. Karen is a wonderful girl, one of the true joys of my life, but there's no pigeonholing her. She went to school at Bennington College in Vermont, and, in many ways, her experiences in such a culturally rich, but very rural environment, stamped her going forward. Her professional choices are a reflection of her peripatetic leanings; she's been a ballet dancer, a dance instructor, a horse groomer and trainer, and, ultimately, a hay farmer. Everything she's done, she's done enormously well, and when she loses interest in an endeavor, she quickly moves on and finds a new passion or develops a new talent. She now lives quite happily on a fifteen hundred–acre ranch in Colorado, where she grows hay and takes care of horses. I will always carry a picture in my mind's eye of Karen as a young dancer—really, the beautiful ways she moved were a wonder!—but, as a parent, I've taken even greater joy in her present pose as a competent, confident adult and a loving daughter doing work she loves and making a good go of it.

Carol was probably my most sentimental child, and yet I never figured her for a businesswoman. She was born on April 9, 1952, and, from the very beginning, she was a lot like her mother: very thorough, opinionated, and big-hearted. She took me completely by surprise one day on a flight to Europe. The flight was a graduation present after she completed her studies at Tulane. She announced that she planned to come to work for the company. Bernice and I had no idea that she wanted to work for Alberto-Culver, and when Carol sprang it on me, she saw that she'd caught me unaware. "If you don't want me to," she said, "I could go to work for one of your competitors." She told me she already had an offer from Colgate-Palmolive.

I thought that was hitting below the belt. "Of course I want you to work with me," I said, and I meant it. At the time, we had approximately three thousand employees worldwide, with sales exceeding one hundred fifty million dollars. and I felt that we surely could accommodate one more salary. Carol, for her part, had it in the back of her mind growing up that she would some day step into this family enterprise, put her own stamp on things, and possibly carve a path for her own children to follow.

I'll never forget the surge of pride I felt one afternoon in 1975 when Carol, all of twenty-three years old and fresh out of school, happened upon the bright idea to make and market a product to help reduce static cling. She'd noticed how difficult it was to keep certain clothes from bunching up with static electricity, and she had our product development people work on a formula to combat the problem. I had no idea she was even pursuing such a thing because, at the time, she reported to a group vice president. I was never quite sure what she did from one day to the next. And yet from this single, bright idea—Carol's single, bright idea!—we developed a product called Static Guard, the first antistatic spray on the market. In the bargain, we created a new product category that we continue to dominate to this day. She went on to become a major force in our new products area, creating brands such as Mrs. Dash, Molly McButter, and Baker's Joy—all still solid sellers.

I always made it a point to express to my children how difficult I had it as a young man. All around me, my friends looked to solid opportunities in this or that family business; their fathers all had companies that gladly would have found a place for them. Me, I had no place to go, and I had to scratch out a living and a place for myself. It was an enormously gratifying, restorative thing to be able to lay that kind of foundation for my own children. As it turned out, such a competitive corporate existence wasn't the thing for Scott or Karen, and that was quite fine with me. But Carol felt that it was a good fit for her, and I was enormously pleased. I don't mean to sound disingenuous about it or to offer a revisionist view of my own history, but the truth of the matter is that I didn't give this prospect any real conscious thought until Carol laid it out for me on that airplane. I suppose I held out the prospect in the back of my mind, and, in some respects, it's possible that the idea of passing the business on to my children influenced many of the decisions I made over the years. But as my three children reached past college into adulthood, it had appeared to Bernice and me that they would reach beyond Alberto-Culver. But, in Carol's case anyway, we couldn't have been more wrong.

Carol married her husband, Howard Bernick, in May, 1976. Howard was born and raised in Canada, where his father was a very successful builder and investor. Howard originally came to work in the United States in investment banking for First Boston, based in Chicago.

To show you the role fate plays, we traditionally spent the holidays at the Arizona Biltmore. Over the years, we came to know

*The Lavins at
the wedding of
their daughter
Carol to
Howard Bernick*

several Canadian families who also regularly spent the holidays
there. One of those families knew the Bernicks quite well, and
when they learned Howard was moving to Chicago, these good
people passed on Carol's number to him. He called, and history
took its course.

Soon enough, I persuaded Howard to move to the Alberto-
Culver company, where he was originally in charge of our acquisitions program. Howard has very strong financial skills, which
nicely balanced Carol's and my entrepreneurial bent. He grew
through the company, becoming president and chief operating
officer in 1986 and chief executive officer in November, 1994.

Now, a word or two about the path their three children have
begun to follow. They're all still quite young, in terms of making

*The Bernick children with their grandparents: Leonard, Lizzie, Craig, Peter, and Bernice*

career choices, and so, for the moment, the prospect of a career at Alberto-Culver is too far in the future really to consider. I will note, though, that for a while, there seemed some chance the business would reach down to the next generation. Carol's oldest, Craig, worked for a time in our marketing department after he graduated from college, and he is now in the media business with a leading international firm. Craig also has shown a lifelong interest in the thoroughbred horse business—our *other* family business. (As I have yet to detail, my passion for the horses led me to a fairly encompassing second career as a breeder of champion thoroughbreds.) Craig and I were always especially close, not least because of our shared love of the horses, and, as a young man, he took a position with a horse farm hoping to learn the business from the ground up, inside and out. Perhaps some day he'll move on to the family horse farm and continue that aspect of the family business, but for now he's getting some real-life business experience.

*The Bernick family: Peter, Lizzie, Craig, Carol, and Howard*

Peter, Carol and Howard's younger son, is currently a student at Vanderbilt University, and he's a big, strapping kid with a variety of interests and talents. He's one of those kids who probably could do anything he wants once he sets his mind to it. Bernice and I have always marveled at the quick way he thinks and at his unusual warmth. Really, I've never met a more caring or more loving child—and I sometimes forget that he's no longer a child. I don't know that Peter's given much serious thought to any kind of career at his early point. For now, his interests run mostly to girls and sports, which is as it should be, don't you think?

Carol's daughter Lizzie, at sixteen, is one of the true lights of my life. Only time will tell if the family business will course through her veins like it did with her mother. Right now, she's just a junior in high school, and she's mad about softball. I'm constantly looking for opportunities to sneak away from the office to catch one of her games. In so doing, I am reminded of the tug and pull I faced as a much younger man, looking to carve out

*Scott Lavin,*
*Leonard and*
*Bernice's son*

some quality time for my own children, to share the touchstone moments of their growing up even as I worked to make the business a success.

The more things change, the more they stay the same, wouldn't you agree?

⟡

Now, I need to spend some time on the saddest chapter of my life—indeed, on the saddest chapter in the life of my family. My boy Scott died of a heart attack on January 12, 1998. It was a devastating turn.

Scott's son Preston was visiting us at the time and was upstairs with Bernice playing gin when I took the horrible phone call. Preston was supposed to go to Los Angeles to see Scott the next morning to begin his search for a college in the United States, when, all of a sudden, we had to face the fact that Scott was gone.

Here one day, gone the next.

I can't tell you what a blow it was to lose a son like that. In the prime of his young life. With everything to look forward to.

*The Lavins's grandson*
*Preston, son of Scott*

Scott was only forty-eight years old, and our only comfort was that he crammed one hundred years of living into the time that he had. All my life, I'd heard people talk about how painful it was to lose a child, and here it hit me full in the face. It tore at my heart. I put down the phone and thought of Bernice and Preston upstairs playing cards. Even as I grieved and faced down this hard, new reality, there loomed a difficult piece of this difficult equation: how to pass the news on to Bernice and Preston. My God, it was the hardest thing I ever had to do in my life, to tell my wife that our son was gone, to tell my grandson that his father was gone. Taking that call was hard enough, but what lay ahead seemed harder still. The walk upstairs was just a few paces, but it felt like miles. To this day, I don't know where or how I found the words, but, somehow, I did. It was such a terrible, traumatic moment. We were all devastated. We called Carol straightaway, and she came right over with her family. Some of our good, lifelong friends came by to offer what comfort and support they could. Karen was out of town and couldn't get to us that evening, but she came as soon as possible. The house began filling up around ten or eleven o'clock that first night, and it was such a protracted, painful evening. I wouldn't wish such a night on anyone. You'll forgive me, dear reader, if it's too difficult to go into any further detail here.

What I can offer, joyfully, is the legacy that Scott left behind. In many ways, it took his sudden death to open our eyes to the kind of generous, boundless spirit he truly was. After he died, we received all kinds of letters from all kinds of people. In each letter, there was something uplifting, something that caught us by surprise, something we hadn't even suspected. We learned that Scott had the warmest heart. We always knew as much, as his warmth related to family, but it was a gratifying revelation to hear of it in these new contexts. Dozens and dozens of letters. From hotel managers where he was fond of staying. From college friends. From variously successful Hollywood types, who'd worked with Scott in one way or another. From people he had known only briefly or fleetingly. In the eyes of these strangers (strangers to *us*, anyway), we saw our son anew. At Scott's memorial service, just to offer an example, I was approached by a young man who told me that he came all the way from Brooklyn to pay his respects. The fellow was dressed in an urban street style that made him look a bit like a hoodlum, but he told me he was a basketball coach working with underprivileged children in a particularly depressed part of the city, and that Scott had been his biggest benefactor. I never knew! Apparently, Scott was out to dinner one night, seated at a table within earshot of this young coach, who was soliciting funds from a potential donor. Scott listened to the fellow's pitch and wrote him a check for ten thousand dollars right there, even though he wasn't the one being solicited. Over the years, he gave whenever the coach called and told him they were scraping bottom.

What a comforting thing it was, to hear that my child moved about with such warmth and caring, that he was loved and admired by people I had never met. That he showed such silent strength and goodness. That he made the kinds of choices you might have made for him. Of course, Scott could be a headstrong kid—each of my children, in their own ways, was fairly head-strong—but it was a great comfort to know that he was held in such high esteem by so many different people for so many different reasons. It wasn't enough to bring him back, but it would have to be enough to keep his memory close going forward.

Scott's son Preston, I wish to mention, is also one of the great lights of my life. He's really blossomed into a fine young man. Like his father before him, he's expressed no abiding interest in the family business, but he's bound for big things, I can tell you that. As I write this, he lives nearby in Chicago, is going to DePaul University, and will graduate soon. He comes over to the house occasionally for dinner. I can't stress how meaningful this close connection is to Bernice and me as we slow down our paces at work and redouble our efforts to keep connected with our children and grandchildren on the home front.

# 7

# Business as Unusual

IN MANY WAYS, THE NUMBERS TELL THE STORY OF OUR RUNAWAY GROWTH at Alberto-Culver as we hit our corporate stride. We were the second largest advertiser of hair-care products in the world by 1963. We reached one hundred million dollars in sales by 1964. We employed two thousand people worldwide by 1966.

But in more compelling ways, the story of our company could be found in the stops and starts along the way, in the occasional departures from the normal course of doing business, and in how we grew accordingly. Consider, for example, the saga we confronted over labor, which, in many respects, mirrored some of the paces other growing businesses were put through during this same period. Recall, throughout the early to middle 1960s, the country at large became more and more pro-labor—coinciding, I suppose, with the civil rights movement and the free, liberal spirit that appeared to rule the land. My thinking in the management and labor area was, and remains, clear: the way a company treats its workforce is the most telling barometer of its forward-thinking abilities. To this end, I always encouraged our top people to ensure that *all* of our employees were well-compensated and treated fairly. Goodness, Bernice and I always felt that those things should be a given, a foundation of any sound business strategy. Too often, our leading American corporations are too willing to eschew the good and welfare of the workforce in favor of other bottom-line concerns. This strikes me as short-sighted and narrow-minded—penny-wise and pound-foolish, to borrow a worn expression—and yet it is the order of the day, the way business gets done. At Alberto-Culver, however, we strove to meet our targets while we focused on our working environment, from top to bottom. With this outlook, it frequently happened that we moved to meet a potential labor problem head-on.

One such occasion stands out in memory. It merits review for the way it illustrates the constant give and take between management and labor, the aggressive posturing of special interest groups which don't always recognize the interests of the people they're meant to watchdog, and the ways a good turn can sometimes come back to bite you in the end.

More than ever before, labor unions were becoming a strong presence in the American workplace, and I knew it was only a matter of time before some union came into our shop and exerted its influence. Early in 1963, as our employee ranks swelled into the thousands, I chose to welcome this prospect rather than fight it. To that end, I went out and looked for a union that would fairly represent our factory employees and treat the resulting negotiation process with management with respect and good will. Like anything else, there are good unions, and there are not-so-good unions. I felt that it made good sense to seek out one of the former. Let me tell you, it wasn't an easy search because even then certain labor unions had developed unsavory reputations for their bullying tactics and such. Nevertheless, I did come across representatives from the Woodworkers Union. They seemed like ethical, reasonable people with a positive track record, and so I invited them to come and meet with our workers and perhaps solicit their representation, if that was something both parties wanted to pursue.

As it happened, the Woodworkers were indeed intrigued by the thought of representing factory workers at a rapidly growing company like Alberto-Culver, and our employees, in turn, expressed interest in having a larger voice to advocate for issues of concern to them. Therefore, union organizers put in motion the long process of gaining the support of our employees, signing a contract, and so forth. The trouble was, as our initiative became public, we soon realized that these weren't the only labor leaders in town. Of course, we fully realized this going in, which was why we reached out to such a decent outfit in the first place, but we hadn't counted on the way reaching out put Alberto-Culver employees "in play" as far as other organizers were concerned.

One morning, as the association with the Woodworkers Union was moving forward—quite positively, I will note—our vice president of human resources came to see me in my office. He informed me that representatives of the Teamsters Union had descended on our facility and begun distributing literature, declaring that they had won the right to represent our people. I was incensed.

"What are you talking about?" I shot back to our vice president, who was in the unfortunate position of being the bearer of bad news.

"Just what I said," he explained. "The Teamsters claim to have organized a group of our employees, and they mean to come in and solicit the rest."

You must remember that for a period of time in Chicago, the Teamsters Local No. 708 reportedly was controlled by an unsavory interest, and, from headlines making our local newspapers, the reports appeared justified. I had no first-hand knowledge as to whether these reports were true, but the Teamsters seemed to leave a negative impression in their wake. They certainly were a difficult organization with which to deal. Plus, I didn't see that we had to deal with them; we had a positive relationship already in place with the Woodworkers Union, and, by all accounts, our people were well represented.

But, like it or not, we *did* have to deal with the Teamsters— and on their terms, apparently. They succeeded in setting up blockades around our headquarters building in Melrose Park, which meant my people couldn't get in or out without running their gauntlet. Moreover, trucks couldn't get into our shipping or receiving bays without interference. After a time, there was hardly any trucking activity at all because, of course, the Teamsters controlled all the truck drivers in the region. It quickly got to the point where this union action cost us thousands of dollars a day, mostly in lost man hours, but also in shipping delays. I wanted the matter resolved, and soon, but, at the same time, I remained mindful of the power and reputation of this particular group. I didn't want to mess with the Teamsters, and I *certainly* didn't want any trouble with the type of people reportedly running them.

Immediately, I asked my attorneys to arrange a meeting with a Teamsters representative, and this fellow came in presenting all types of documents meant to prove that he had the support of our employees, and offering a sweetheart come-on deal to gain the support of our management team. The fellow's name was Louis Pike, and he had a reputation as long as the outfit he represented.

"We've already got a union," I said, after giving all these papers a cursory look. "We can't deal with you."

"Oh, but you have to," Pike insisted.

"Like I said," I repeated, "we've got a union."

"Well, throw them out," Pike said. "Your people want to deal with us."

The sweetheart deal Louis Pike proposed included all kinds of concessions—reduced wages, and so forth—which, I realized, of course, was only a one-time, short-term thing. Still, I felt I had no choice but to look over the proposal. "This contract is only for one year," I noted, when I had read through the union's terms. "What happens after that?"

"Well," the representative said, "after that, we renegotiate."

By *renegotiate* I assumed he meant he would strong-arm us into far more onerous terms. If I took this one little piece of candy this year, our heads would be chopped off the next. Naturally, I turned Louis Pike down, and almost as soon as I chased him from my office, I was on the phone with a fellow from the National Labor Relations Board in Washington, but he wasn't much help. I actually went down to Washington to see this man, but, at that time, the NLRB was extremely pro-labor, reflecting the mood of the country, and this bureaucrat wasn't inclined to see things our way. The fact that *our* way seemed to me to be the right way, the just way, didn't much matter.

"What is it you're looking for?" the NLRB representative asked.

"Well," I said, "I want the opportunity for my people to at least have an election. Let them decide which union they want to represent them."

As I recall, this meeting took place in the summer of 1963, several months after our initial business with organizers from the Woodworkers Union, and some weeks into this ugliness with the Teamsters. Regrettably, the NLRB was unable to intervene, and, before I returned to Chicago, I stopped in to see a well-known Washington D.C. attorney named Clark Clifford. I laid out my story, after which Mr. Clifford said he would be happy to represent us in the matter—for a one-hundred-thousand-dollar retainer. I thought that was a little steep to get to the bottom of these shady doings, so I thanked the lawyer for his time.

Next, I reached out to one of our senators, the esteemed Everett McKinley Dirksen. Senator Dirksen had represented the fine state of Illinois for almost four decades, first as a congressman and, beginning in 1950, as a United States senator. He was a close friend of W. Russell Arrington, one of our original backers and himself a state senator. Senator Dirksen and I had met each other a few times over the years at fundraisers, dinners, and so forth, and I felt that he would give us a fair hearing. At the very least, I hoped he could offer some sound advice, and so I retold the tale to the senator as well. As I did, for the third time that day, I became even more outraged at the bullying tactics of the

Teamsters. It had become clear to our human resources people that the Teamsters were attempting to organize our entire plant. They had a long-range plan that would have brought our chemists and our marketing people into their shop, along with our factory workers and shipping clerks; virtually all of our employees beneath management levels would have to join the union. Apparently, the Teamsters had targeted a number of companies, like International Harvester and Motorola. At the time, we were the smallest company in their sights, so they thought to move in on the upstart Alberto-Culver first and hope their other targets fell into place after that. Also, our human resources people caught a great deal of the unrest outside our plant on camera—Teamsters slashing tires and threatening everybody from factory workers to the management team. I reported how, since the Teamsters controlled virtually all trucking business in our area, we were having a devil of a time with deliveries; when we tried to hire non-union drivers, a series of violent incidents followed which were meant to thwart any such moves in the future.

I shared all of this with Senator Dirksen, who listened with great interest, and when I was through, he gave the matter his serious consideration. "Leonard," he said, after a long pause for reflection, "I think I might be able to help you. Why don't you take a walk for about an hour or so. When you come back, we can talk about our next move."

I thought this sounded promising. After weeks spent reaching out to one politician or bureaucrat or another, I felt as if I was finally going to get some positive result on this troubling matter or at least some resolution. So I took a walk, as the senator advised, and, upon my return to his office, I was told he would be with me shortly. As I waited, a short, busy, little man with a briefcase was escorted into Senator Dirksen's office. I didn't think anything of it until about a half an hour later when I was called back into the same office and introduced to the same individual. I learned only the fellow's name and the fact that he was an attorney in some sort of position to speak on the matter with some authority. Once again, I went through the saga with labor and the unions, and, once again, I sought to present the facts in a straightforward, objective manner.

When I was finished, the gentleman asked me what I was looking for to close the issue. "It's like I've been saying all along," I reiterated. "I just want our people to have a chance to decide their fates for themselves. Let them vote on it. If they want to go with the Teamsters, okay. If they want to stay with the Woodworkers, okay, but let's have a fair election."

With this, the attorney looked at the senator, and the senator looked back at the attorney, and each man appeared to flash the other a nod of agreement.

"When would you like the election?" the attorney asked, after this brief, unspoken exchange.

I remembered from consultations with our labor attorneys that under state and federal labor laws, management was entitled to speak directly to employees on pending union consideration up until two days before a posted election. I thought it would be wise to take full advantage of such a provision, given the circumstances. "Give us a month," I said, not really asking, but thinking out loud that thirty days should be plenty of time to canvas our people. I may have stated that all I was looking for was a fair election, but, in truth, I wanted a fighting chance to ensure a positive outcome—that is, to vote the Teamsters off our property.

Once again, the senator and the attorney exchanged looks and came to some tacit accord; the one-month waiting period was agreed to all around, and the attorney shook our hands and left the senator's office. When he was gone and the door closed behind him, Senator Dirksen informed me that the gentleman was the personal attorney for one of the most powerful men in the labor movement, someone who was attempting to curry favor with Bobby Kennedy, who was, at the time, the United States attorney general. Senator Dirksen explained that he had agreed to prevail on Kennedy to consider a problem with the attorney's client.

It struck me then, as it does now in the retelling, that it was a fairly high-level deal on behalf of an operation that only eight years earlier was conducted from a Los Angeles storefront with a couple of oil drums out back. But we came a long way in a rather short space of time. Indeed, we came far enough that our elected representative in the United States Senate and the attorney general (the brother of the president, no less!) became involved in matters that concerned our interests. I thought to myself, okay, Leonard, you've done good.

But all we'd won with this agreement was the opportunity to let our people decide the matter, and there was still a month of canvassing and such before our election. I thanked the senator for his considerable help and returned home to lay the groundwork with our human resources people to ensure a fair election. Hopefully, it would be one with a favorable result, but I had not counted on the Teamsters' continued presence at our plant over the next weeks. They continued with their pickets, their blockades, and their other strong-arming tactics. We still couldn't ship or receive goods with any regularity. There was no blatant or outward harassment of our people as there had been prior to this hard-won concession in Senator Dirksen's office, but there was still a good deal of unpleasantness and disruptive behavior on the part of these shady organizers. We felt that there was nothing we could do about it other than to ensure that our people were treated fairly *inside* our building, that their working environment remain positive, and that a healthy line of positive communication was kept open with our employees.

Toward the end of the thirty-day waiting period, I gave a speech to our assembled workforce. I spoke extemporaneously and detailed some of the initiatives that we enacted over the years to treat our employees fairly. I highlighted our efforts to promote from within and detailed some of the progressive, pro-labor policies that were already in place at Alberto-Culver without any union intervention. It was, I thought, a positive speech, but, as I spoke, I realized that I needed a big kicker. After all, you can't really rally the troops without a big kicker, right? So I put things as plainly as I could. If you want things to stay as they are, I said, vote against the Teamsters. If you want the Teamsters, okay, you'll get the Teamsters. "Either way," I concluded, "we'll have a big party after the election. However it turns out, we'll get things off on the right note, and we'll all be friends."

Well, the election finally rolled around on the calendar, and there was a great deal of tension in the air. I felt that we made a strong argument for sticking with our present situation and demonstrated how an association with Teamsters might create a tense atmosphere. From our informal polling, it seemed that our voices were heard, but we couldn't be certain until the votes were in. As the votes were recorded and then tallied by independent auditors, Bernice and I sat with some of our people and some of the Teamsters representatives. We were all in the same room waiting on the result. As I mentioned, the head of the Teamsters effort in our plant was a fellow named Louis Pike, and he was well known in Chicago for his harassing style. I didn't like having to deal with him to this point, and I hoped I wouldn't have to deal with him going forward. Really, this was an unpleasant fellow— nothing more than a big bully with a reputation I did not like.

As the votes were counted, one of our human resources people whispered to me that the Woodworkers, which basically represented the status quo, were running ahead of the Teamsters in the tally by a seven to one margin. I leaned over to Bernice and whispered the same, and she took it to mean that our side surely would win. In most respects, she never was one to count all her chickens before they hatched, but she was so sick and tired of the strong-arming and the nastiness evidenced by the Teamsters that she couldn't help but speak her mind. The news of the margin presented her with her first opportunity to do so from a position of strength. She sought out Louis Pike across the room and caught his attention.

"When this is all over," she said, loudly enough for everyone in the room to hear, "you get your people and get out of here. We've had enough of you, you know."

Louis Pike was a mean-spirited man, and he wasn't used to being spoken to in this way—and by a woman! Pike turned red in the face and shot back some invective or other, and then he threatened Bernice in his bullying way. But even he could see that the tide had turned against him. His threats, which at one point might have scared the daylights out of Bernice, suddenly rang hollow.

Let me tell you, I never was more proud of my wife than I was at just that moment. The way she refused to cower in the face of such bullying tactics, the way she had the pluck to say what everyone on our management team had been thinking—these were good and wonderful things. I counted myself extremely lucky to have her on my side.

In the end, the Teamsters were voted down by about that same seven to one margin, and I was good to my word about the big party to follow. There was a fine celebration at the Palmer House, open bar and all that, with dancing and so forth. I even hired the famous singer Dorothy Dandridge to perform, and she was absolutely marvelous. Naturally, all these arrangements were made prior to the election in order to secure the room and the caterer, but it wouldn't have been much of a party if the Teamsters had won. There'd have been nothing to celebrate, right? In hindsight, I suspect that I might have asked Miss Dandridge to accept her fee and go home without performing because those Teamsters didn't deserve such a sweet-voiced performer, but, happily, we all were treated to her singular talent. After all, our people had everything to celebrate, and a moment such as this called for nothing less than the very best.

A few years later, in 1967, Jimmy Hoffa, international head of the Teamsters Union, was sentenced to thirteen years in federal prison at Lewisburg, Pennsylvania, on charges of jury tampering, pension fraud, and conspiracy. President Nixon commuted his sentence after only four years, though. His power was demonstrated by the fact that, during his time in prison, he continued as the head of the Teamsters. By now, of course, Jimmy Hoffa's name has lapsed into American lore for his famous disappearance in 1975. However, whenever I hear Hoffa's name or talk turns to his whereabouts or his fate, I think back to his powerful union's failed effort to organize our troops all those years ago. Thinking back, I am reminded that it is often the good energy you put out that cloaks you in good fortune going forward. We easily could have shrunk from the Teamsters and allowed them to change the tone and the direction of our company, but it was too important to me, Bernice, and the other good people on our board and in management to maintain the productive family atmosphere that was in place when we started out. I can say with some certainty that the Teamsters would have destroyed that atmosphere; indeed, their mere presence on our property was so disruptive that it nearly eroded all those years of goodwill. But, ultimately, that goodwill paid great dividends for Alberto-Culver. It enabled us to chase the Teamsters from our midst and return the Woodworkers Union to the fore, which allowed our workers to do what it was they signed on to do in the first place.

The lesson here, I've always thought, is never to take your business relationships for granted, and the most important business relationship will always be the one between management and labor. Without a solid foundation of mutual trust and respect, you'll never make a good go of anything.

◦━━◦

With our house in order, I was free once again to get back to my roots in the business—that is, to travel the world haunting drug stores, beauty salons, and specialty outlets to scout out new products or product categories. Our early successes almost always flowed from taking on items developed elsewhere, and the search for those items was never-ending and far-reaching. It could have been all-consuming, as well, were we not content to build our business one brand at a time.

More and more, as our company grew, these "fact-finding" tours took me overseas, and on a tour of a European drug and convenience store, I noticed an item on the shelves I never even had considered. Why? Well, I'd never imagined the need. It was a vaginal deodorant spray, and it struck me then as the most marvelously revolutionary product idea I'd heard of in the longest time. I took a package off the shelf and considered the implications, and, as I did, I realized that our business was really one of perception. It was a spray powder in a delicate, feminine package, and the mere fact of its existence suggested that it met a need for some women. I'd never heard of such a thing, but the Europeans were always a step or two ahead of us ugly Americans in matters of such refinement, right?

I bought a couple packages of the stuff and shipped them home to our chemists at the lab with instructions to look into coming up with our own formula for a similar product. Well, two or three weeks later, I was back in Chicago, eager to meet with our product development people. I spoke with the chemist assigned to the project. "How soon can we have this thing ready?" I asked, with great enthusiasm. Really, I felt sure we could do great things with this item.

"Well, Mr. Lavin," the chemist cautioned, "we made a few samples, but I don't think it's something you'll want to pursue."

I hadn't counted on this. "Why is that?" I wanted to know.

"There's really no need for it," the chemist allowed, with great candor. "It smells nice and all, but it doesn't really do anything."

I explained to him how it was all a matter of perception and self-confidence. Still, our head chemist resisted. "We can make something," he said. "It'll be a good product and have a nice smell, but it's like I told you before, Mr. Lavin. It won't really *do* anything."

"Make it anyway," I said, determined to follow my gut—or at least the Europeans' lead. The item was selling over there, and it wasn't my style to try and "put one over" on the American public, but I didn't see what I was trying to do as deceptive in any way. We would make this nice feminine spray. Women would use it and feel good about themselves. They'd smell nice and move about with a special confidence because they knew they smelled nice. It was a delicate issue, to be sure, but when you broke it down, the entire cosmetics industry was built on items we could do without. We weren't selling food or water or air. We made and marketed niceties, nonessentials, in terms of basic survival, but nevertheless indispensable tools in terms of our shared self-esteem. We helped people feel better about themselves. If a woman felt this product met a need, she'd go out and try our product. What she'd find by trying it would be a pleasant-smelling, satisfying spray that was easy to use and would leave her feeling a little more sure of herself.

And so we continued with our development of the item, even though our people still weren't sold on the idea. We did some initial testing, and the results weren't very encouraging. I still looked to the category's success in Europe as an indication of the success that was waiting for us at home. I was pretty adamant about it, I'll admit. It wasn't like me to go against our development team like this, but on this one I was firm. We would take this item to market and see what happened. If I was proven wrong in the marketplace, then I would take full responsibility for my stubbornness. If I was proven right? Well, it was my job to be right.

Our people came up with a name—FDS, for Feminine Deodorant Spray—and a soft, tasteful package, then it fell to us to figure how to advertise it. This was 1966, and we couldn't advertise the product on the radio. We certainly couldn't get it on television. Nowadays, of course, there are commercials for sanitary napkins, condoms, vaginal douches, and all kinds of things, but, back then, this was new ground. There were no broadcast networks willing to help us get our sensitive message out, so we turned to print. Our advertising agency developed a series of smart, subtle print ads to run in various women's magazines such as *Redbook* and *McCall's*. The ad copy wasn't as straightforward as I would have liked, but our marketing people insisted that the American consumer wasn't ready for a direct hard sell on an item such as this, so I went along with the approach. You really had to read between the lines to get what it was our spray accomplished, but the message was clear: buy our product, use it discerningly, and you will feel fresh and feminine all over.

We were getting ready to launch the product in targeted markets when I learned that Warner-Lambert, one of our major competitors in the category of hygiene products, was readying a similar item they called Pristine, which they were currently testing in Atlanta and San Diego. Johnson and Johnson, we also found out, had its own vaginal deodorant in the works. Realize, we were small potatoes next to these big boys, and the only competitive advantage we'd enjoy in a head-to-head battle for market share would come in beating them to the punch. I immediately hired our own market research company and put them to work trying to read the market response to the Pristine test in Atlanta and San Diego. It wasn't the most sporting approach, but it was a sound strategy: if we could determine public response to the Warner-Lambert test, we could tweak our own campaign going forward. Johnson and Johnson wasn't planning a test, as far as we could determine, so once we collected our data on Pristine, we went ahead with our FDS launch. The only way to beat these guys, I figured, was to go national with our new product, and so we did.

It was a slow start, getting this thing off the ground without the benefit of a radio or television campaign, but we began to develop a following. We had no trouble getting the spray into stores. We were a hot outfit at the time, and outlets were eager to take on our new products, so there was no surprise there. The surprise, really, was how painstakingly slow it was to get the word out the old-fashioned way, through print and word-of-mouth, after becoming accustomed to the immediate results of a broadcast campaign. We very quickly became the market leader in what was still a nascent market, but I was anxious to make a big splash with this item and never let up on the television front. It was only a matter of time, I knew, before one of the big networks took on a feminine product such as this, so I had our people prepare a television commercial that I could take out to some of the bigger independent stations around the country. I hoped that I could find a maverick station manager willing to put it on the air. Sure enough, that's just what happened at a midwestern network affiliate. Independent stations were free to carry network or local programming and to supplement network advertising with their own local advertising, and we finally got one local station to accept our ad. And, after that first station, there came another. And another. And with each airing of one of our commercials, sales really boomed in the surrounding area. Television, once again, was the marketing tool of the century. This incidence demonstrated that the medium could create demand for a product most people didn't even think they needed.

Ultimately, with all those local network affiliates carrying our ads, I was able to convince Leonard Goldenson at ABC, Bob Kintner at NBC, and Bill Paley at CBS to carry our spots on their daytime shows. Soon enough, Warner-Lambert and Johnson and Johnson outspent us on the advertising front, but they never could make up for the ground they lost with our running head start. Our FDS product was the clear market leader, and that would have been the end of the story were it not for the intervention of a well-connected special interest group that nearly derailed our product. In fact, for a time, that's just what happened: FDS sales went from a steep rise to a flatline virtually overnight. It was some time before we started moving the product again in any kind of significant way.

Here's what happened. One Sunday, some time after the launch of our national television campaign to promote FDS, I was spending a relaxing morning at home with Bernice and the children. It was my habit in those days to read as much of the Sunday paper as I possibly could before family commitments pulled me away. That morning, I came across an item in the news section that sent me reeling. A spokesperson for the Food and Drug Administration came out with a report that found the compound hexachlorophene to be potentially hazardous when used in certain products under certain conditions. Now, hexachlorophene was one of the basic ingredients in the FDS admixture, so I naturally was concerned. In fact, the FDA press release in the newspaper story singled out our FDS as one of the generally available consumer products made with hexachlorophene. Virtually overnight, our sales went into a tailspin. The FDA had not yet banned the compound—that happened in the days ahead— but it set off all kinds of red flags so that no one wanted to touch our product.

That Monday morning, I was in with our chemists, consulting on ways to reformulate the product without hexachlorophene. This was an enormous problem, as far as our bottom line was concerned. Here we had the beginning of a runaway success, a very profitable item, and this single FDA press release cut all the momentum from our sales. Even with a reformulation to bring the product into FDA compliance, we'd suffered a tremendous blow to the product's image, from which the item might never recover. We were devastated, especially since we had done our own internal testing and determined that the product was absolutely and completely safe. I would have used it myself, if I'd had the right body parts.

The head of our laboratories at the time was a very respected Chicago scientist, and, at his urging, we confronted the FDA directly, demanding to see the agency's research and to have a chance to present our own. We had done all kinds of testing on the item, and for the agency suddenly to announce that our main ingredient was harmful and under review was extremely troubling.

Well, our FDA attorney had a difficult time getting an appointment, so I called our new senator, Charles Percy, who was just beginning his first of three terms as a United States senator from Illinois. I must say, Senator Percy was fairly wishy-washy in offering his assistance. All I asked was for him to see if he could get someone at the agency to respond to our calls for an appointment, and he saw it as a call for influence. "Leonard," he said, in putting me off, "I'm not going to interfere on something like this. This is the Food and Drug Administration."

"I'm not asking for you to interfere, Senator," I said. "We just need a little help in setting up a meeting. We're an Illinois company. I'm one of your constituents. Our people seem to be unable to arrange a hearing, so I thought you could push things along."

After a good deal of back and forth, Senator Percy agreed to push for a meeting, but he did so with a caveat: "Whatever happens, Leonard," he said, "you can't use my name."

I had no intention of using his name, and of course I didn't, but I have no qualms about using it here.

A meeting was set for some weeks hence, and all during that time, the sales of our reformulated FDS floundered. Also during that time, the FDA banned the use of hexachlorophene outright, and this second wave of negative publicity made our marketing efforts that much harder. It seemed we'd never get out from under the public relations mess of this hexachlorophene scare without some formal explanation from the FDA, and I had our FDA attorney and chief chemist on the case, preparing our files and so forth.

We collected file cabinets worth of research and test results and sent copies of those files on ahead to Washington. We wanted to do a thorough job of it because we felt strongly we were in the right on this issue.

I went with our head chemist and our FDA attorney to the agency's offices, and the three of us were escorted into a small conference room, where we were told to wait. About fifteen minutes later, a group of eight or nine lab-coated administrators filed in, along with a smattering of civilian types, and our group went into our pitch. We presented our research, complete with charts and graphs and so forth, and at the end of our presentation, our attorney quite reasonably asked if we might now hear some of the agency's findings that presumably ran counter to ours. At this, the doctor who was leading the FDA team gave the floor to one of the people who had accompanied him into the room—a woman. I was somewhat surprised by this turn, but I held my tongue as this woman ripped into us for promoting a product that was demeaning to women, superfluous, and, very likely, dangerous as well.

At one point, I could keep silent no longer. "What are you talking about?" I shot back. "This product is in no way demeaning to women, and it's certainly not dangerous. We came here to show you our research and to look over yours. We're as concerned as everyone in this room about the implications of hexachlorophene, and we mean to answer those concerns. Tell me, what does your research show?"

"Well," this woman managed, "we haven't done any research."

I couldn't believe my ears—indeed, at first, I thought I hadn't heard this woman accurately. "Excuse me?" I said.

"That's just it, Mr. Lavin," she continued. "We didn't feel any research is necessary. As a member of the National Organization of Women (NOW), I know this product is demeaning to women. It doesn't belong on the market. That is our contention."

My mouth was open so wide at this point you could have put a basketball in there; if I had false teeth, they would have fallen out. I was astonished—and too flabbergasted to say anything that might help our case.

Our attorney took up the argument at this point. He castigated everyone present over this startling revelation, telling them in no uncertain terms that they had destroyed a product for no good reason, causing a struggling company to lose millions of dollars in lost revenues and opportunities simply because they didn't like what the product represented.

That encounter was the most outrageous example of influence-peddling I'd ever seen, and what was especially galling was the way that those women coerced the FDA into banning a substance that had a great many other uses as well. At that time, hexachlorophene was one of the leading germicides used in hospitals to combat infections, and, according to all reports, it was completely safe. And here it was, banned simply because we had chosen to use it in a product that these loud women found offensive.

I was furious, but I knew enough to keep quiet. I let the attorney battle it out on our behalf, but all we managed was an empty victory. The FDA rescinded its ban on hexachlorophene in hospitals and for other medicinal uses, but we still were banned from using it in our product, and we certainly never recouped any of our lost revenues. (And believe me, with the successful launch we enjoyed with FDS, those lost revenues were certainly considerable!) We thought about filing some sort of legal action to string up those people for what our team felt was an obvious abuse of power, but we decided to take the high road. We stuck to our plans to reformulate and regroup. Besides, for all our early successes, we didn't have the kind of deep pockets such a lawsuit surely would require, and now that we had to answer to our shareholders as well as to our board and our bottom line, such a move didn't seem prudent.

And so we moved ahead, looking to rebuild the FDS brand to see if we could get the item back to where it was before the FDA went on its NOW-backed attack. And, slowly, we did. We reformulated the product, made a new commercial, and went back on the air to reach consumers. And the public responded. Slowly, they responded one market at a time. I couldn't justify going back out with a national campaign, so we made some spot television buys, beginning in Philadelphia and moving gradually into other, bigger markets until finally it made sense to go wide once more.

Looking back, the entire controversy strikes me yet again as a blatant abuse of office. I don't fault the women at NOW for taking the stand that they did because they're entitled to their opinion, and I suppose that they're also entitled to reach out for whatever support they can find. But, in my opinion, the FDA officials showed an egregious disregard for their positions by caving to the demands of these women. The lesson here—there's *always* a lesson—is that you can't always fight City Hall, but sometimes you can stay the course, stick to your guns, and hope that City Hall shrinks from the battle before you run out of resources.

Another lesson? Never underestimate the influence of a woman scorned—dubiously or otherwise.

⚜

The FDS controversy over the hexachlorophene wasn't our first run-in with the Food and Drug Administration, and this seems a good spot to relate a previous encounter with the agency. I'm flashing back a bit and upsetting the chronology somewhat, but indulge me for the next few pages. Early in our history, back when our Alberto VO5 hairdressing product helped to cement our reputation as a leading manufacturer of hair care and other personal items, I received a "cease and desist" letter from the FDA telling me that our lead product was deceptively packaged. We had to pull the item from shelves within ten days or face criminal penalties.

Normally, in the course of doing business subject to various government regulations, you're given some opportunity to correct a violation, answer a complaint, or otherwise defend your action before receiving something as firm and final as a "cease and desist" notice. Here, though, we were presented with no recourse but to follow the agency's ruling and recall the product, even though to do so would have cost us a small fortune. Plus, from my perspective, there was no cause for the action in the first place. The crux of the FDA claim was that our Alberto VO5 hair-dressing tube was too small relative to the box in which it was packaged and that, by outward appearances, the item appeared to contain far more product than it actually did. Somehow, we were misleading the public with this deception.

I thought, what nonsense! Was the tube smaller than the box that contained it? Absolutely. The thing wouldn't have fit if it had been the same size! But it was printed right on the box how many ounces each tube contained. If we sold the tube on a stand-alone basis, without a boxed-sleeve for protection, it never would have held its shape. Think of it: when was the last time you bought a tube of toothpaste without the tube prepackaged into a box of some kind? Sure, we left some room in the box for a flier or a coupon, which we folded over the tube before inserting it. There was additional room to allow the tube to move about during shipping without becoming squished and unsightly, but the practice had never raised an eyebrow before we received this notice.

As I've indicated, the most troubling aspect of this turn was that there seemed to be no recourse. The FDA already ruled on the matter, and we had no choice but to withdraw the item in its present package. The cost and nuisance to recall a small item like our hairdressing were enormous, but we really had no choice. Still, I wasn't about to accept a ruling like this without a fight, and even as we made an effort to comply with the order, I made my displeasure known. I reached out to an interesting fellow I'd befriended named Dynamite Sokol, a political reporter for the old *Chicago American* newspaper. He was a little guy with big clout, which, I suppose, was how he got his nickname. Chicago was a really political town, then as now, and Sokol knew every-body. He was close with our mayor, Richard J. Daley (father of our current mayor, Richard M. Daley), and every local politician and restaurateur of whom you could think. If there was an angle to be played in the city of Chicago, in the state of Illinois, or in the wide world beyond, you could be sure Sokol knew how to play

it. He was a good friend, and when I told him about the FDA
action, he shared my outrage. Right away, he put me in touch
with an Illinois congressman named John C. Kluczynski. This fellow wasn't my congressman at all, but Sokol suggested that he
might be inclined to look into the matter on my behalf. Sokol
went over to the congressman's campaign office personally, and
I received an appointment immediately at the congressman's office in Washington.

Congressman Kluczynski was a rather large Polish man and a
real powerhouse. Like our mutual friend, Dynamite Sokol, he was
plugged into everything. I told the congressman the story of the
"cease and desist" letter, and he was nearly as riled about it as I
was. I even showed him the letter because he didn't believe the
story at first. He'd never heard of a government agency acting in
this way on a matter such as this. He felt, as I did, that if the FDA
wanted us to do something about our packaging, they should have
presented us with a reasonable timetable to come into compliance—and only after they had first given us an opportunity to explain our present packaging.

"Leonard," he finally said, after giving the matter some
thought. "I'm going to help you. Come with me."

With that, he escorted me into the bowels of Congress to a
small train that ran between some of the office buildings. I never
knew that such a setup existed, but there it was. The trains were
all open cars, almost like coal cars, and they ran quietly along
narrow lengths of track. I imagine that, at one time, they were
considered a real time-saver, especially in the dead of winter. We
rode along in this way to another office building, and the congressman took me upstairs to see Congressman Sam Rayburn of
Texas, who, at that time, was the speaker of the house. Kluczynski
told the speaker that I was a constituent of his (which wasn't entirely true) who was being improperly threatened by the FDA, and
Speaker McCormack seemed to share our indignation.

"Tell him your story, Leonard," Congressman Kluczynski
said.

So I told him my story. It was a pattern I repeated several times more throughout the day. From the speaker's office, we moved on to the chairman of the House Appropriations Committee, and, following that, we paid a visit to Senator George H. Bender of Ohio. At each stop, we left with promises to look into the matter and offers of whatever help their office could muster. I'd been to Washington before and met with my share of congressmen and senators, but I'd never been treated to such an inside, up-close display of how things really got done in that town. I'd always known, on some level, that our government was made up of a series of "old boys networks," and I saw some of that in play.

Next, we moved to the Office of the Vice President, Richard M. Nixon. I've already recounted my tale of a later, more personal exchange with the former president, but we first met in his office on that whirlwind day in 1958, when Congressman Kluczynski pulled strings for me. Naturally, the vice president was a busy man, but he made time for us, even though we were unannounced. He, too, offered to help in what ways he could offer it.

Finally, back in the congressman's office, we placed a call to Arthur S. Fleming, who, at that time, was the head of the Department of Health, Education, and Welfare, under which the FDA operated. We asked to be put on the gentleman's calendar for breakfast the following morning.

"I'd be happy to meet with you, Congressman," came the reply, "but what is the nature of the meeting?"

"I have a constituent here by the name of Leonard Lavin," he reported into the phone. "He runs the Alberto-Culver Company in Chicago, and he's in receipt of a cease and desist order from the FDA I'd like to discuss with you. I'll bring him with me to breakfast, if that's alright with you."

"That'll be fine," Mr. Fleming said, and we made plans to meet the following morning at seven o'clock in the congressional dining room.

Congressman Kluczynski hung up the phone and turned to me. "Everything's arranged," he said. "Why don't you go back to your hotel and meet me for dinner tonight at the Army-Navy Club?" he suggested. "Is six-thirty okay with you?"

"Six-thirty's fine, Congressman," I said. Of course, I had no idea where the Army-Navy Club was or what I could expect to happen there, but, at that point, I felt I was merely along for the ride. The congressman had introduced me to so many influential people in such a short stretch of time that I couldn't imagine what lay in store that evening, and I couldn't think how all the exchanges were going to help us in the matter of our supposedly deceptive packaging. But I did as I was told. I went back to the hotel, found the location of the Army-Navy Club, and rested up for what I thought might be a long night.

Six-thirty came around on the clock, and I taxied over to the Army-Navy Club, appropriately attired for the evening. Who should we meet but Congressman Rayburn, Senator Bender, Vice President Nixon, and, of course, a number of other Washington movers and shakers. It was a regular who's who of the Beltway, and we were smack in its middle. Each time I was reintroduced to one of the officials I met earlier that day, the conversation went much the same:

"Good to see you again, Mr. Lavin."

"Anything I can do to help."

"Any progress on that matter with the FDA?"

"Let my office know if there's anything you need."

And so on, right down the line. To a man, these elected officials couldn't have been more solicitous or eager to please—and I was wise enough to know that their largesse had everything to do with their various relationships with Congressman Kluczynski and nothing at all to do with me.

The dinner itself was a fine, formal affair, complete with tuxedoed butlers and such, but the main event was a poker game, to which these esteemed gentlemen retired following the meal. One by one, they took off their jackets, loosened their ties, rolled up their sleeves, and got down to the real business of the evening. I was something of a poker player myself, but I didn't presume to sit in on this one. In fact, I wasn't invited to play, but Congressman Kluczynski pointed to a chair just off to the side and suggested I grab a seat and get comfortable. "Who knows," he joked, "you might learn something."

What a priceless scene! These half-dozen or so enormously powerful men unwinding after a hard day attending to the nation's business, playing poker with all the brio we enjoyed in our own games back home. Cussing each other out, calling each other's bluff, razzing on whoever it was who couldn't seem to catch a break. Just a regular bunch of guys drinking, smoking, and playing cards, only every once in a while, I'd catch a line like, "Mr. Vice President, you're full of shit!" and realize that, of course, this was no regular bunch of guys.

At precisely eleven-thirty, the butler returned to the room, announced the time, and began collecting all the empty whiskey bottles and emptying the ashtrays. One of the congressmen collected the chips, and the men reknotted their ties, pulled out their cuffs, put on their jackets, and disappeared into the Washington night looking every bit the respectable official. It was, indeed, a rare and memorable evening, made more so by the fact that I was at least peripherally involved.

At seven o'clock the following morning, these same men were none the worse for all the whiskey and poker of the night before. Once again, the same cast of characters paraded past our breakfast table as we sat with the head of Health, Education, and Welfare and a couple of his aides. "Good morning, Leonard," I heard. (After the familiarity of the night before, I graduated from Mr. Lavin to Leonard.)

"Good to see you."

"Be sure to let me know if I could be of help."

Even Vice President Nixon made it a point to stop by our table, and surely all these well-wishes from such a powerful group of Washington players left Secretary Fleming feeling that his agency might have picked on the wrong guy on the wrong issue. It was quite something to see the ways in which this man's attitude shifted as the breakfast progressed. He couldn't have been more solicitous by the end of the meal. He finally turned to his assistant, who had accompanied him to the breakfast meeting, and suggested that together they should take a second look at the Alberto-Culver file when they got back to the office to make sure the FDA had taken the proper course of action.

And that was that. I walked Congressman Kluczynski back to his office, and, in parting, he said to me, "Go home, Leonard. Forget about it. Go about your business."

"What about the cease and desist order?" I wanted to know. "I don't want to face any penalties by ignoring it."

"You won't be ignoring it," he reasoned. "You've taken care of it. You've had this meeting. Everything will be fine."

I thanked the congressman for his time and extra effort and returned home to Chicago, scratching my head all the way over the marvelously strange experiences of the past twenty-four hours. A few days later, the congressman called me at my office with the final update on the matter. "The FDA has rescinded its order," he happily announced. He told me his office would send along corroborating documents, as well as a copy of the file that had put us under suspicion in the first place. When some of his poker-playing friends came up for re-election, I enthusiastically wrote out a few healthy checks from my own personal account for their campaigns.

The footnote to this story came in the fine print. In reading over the FDA files when they arrived at my office a few dates later, I learned that the investigation into the packaging stemmed from a complaint lodged by the Helene Curtis company, one of Alberto-Culver's principal competitors. In just a few short years, an upstart company had cut deeply into sales of Helene Curtis's hairdressing line, and I suppose it was that company's way of striking back. It couldn't compete with us in the marketplace, so it looked to other means to tilt the advantage back in its direction.

Naturally, I was reminded of this initial complaint years later, when our company was once again caught in the FDA's cross-hairs following the complaint of those activists from NOW. This first time, though, it wasn't a woman scorned who turned out to be the source of all our troubles, but a woman beaten at her own game.

⌐⬝⬝⬝⬝⬝⬝¬

I want to highlight a slight detour we took in the evolution of our business toward the end of the 1960s. It was a shift I never would have anticipated back when I was first charting our course for growth, but it was one that clearly transformed our company going forward. The turn nicely illustrates how it is that you sometimes lose sight of your initial goal, and how if you're not careful, the big picture can be made smaller by a kind of tunnel vision.

I'll explain. See, in those days, in the beauty supply industry, there were two distinct lines of attack. You sold directly to the consumer through retail outlets like drug stores and discount chains, or you placed your products through salon owners and licensed beauticians, who, in turn, ordered them from a wholesaler or a regional sales representative working directly for the manufacturer. The practice, then as now, was to position an item for one market or another, rarely both.

We made our mark early on the retail side of the business, with an emphasis on value-priced items, but there was no denying that there was money to be made on the salon or professional side. We had a professional division that sold to the wholesalers on a fits-and-starts basis, but the beauty professionals had only a lukewarm interest in our items. They loved the VO5 hairdressing because it was such a unique item, but there was a perception that our hairsprays for beauty salons were at the low end of the market and, therefore, undesirable for customers of high-end salons. Compounding this perception was the fact that this particular segment of the business never held any real appeal to me and seemed too clunky and layered for our low-cost products. Part of my disinterest, I'll confess here, was because it was a part of the business I didn't truly understand. I was a salesman, first and foremost, and getting the American public to respond to a new item or a new product category was at the heart of almost everything we did at Alberto-Culver. But even when I could get my head around the fact that there were ways to expand our business that weren't necessarily product-driven, I was confounded by the too-many-mouths-to-feed aspect of the beauty industry's professional side. I never felt that there was enough profit to go around if we offered the consumer a fair value.

Say you were a salon owner, and you wanted to carry a certain line of products for your customers. You'd be visited by a "professional products" wholesaler, who was looking to place the wares of a number of manufacturers into different specialty shops and beauty parlors around the country. You'd look through a big catalog of available items, perhaps sample a few, and then you'd place your order. The wholesaler would write the order and send it back to his office, where it would be processed by the credit department. Then it would move to shipping, where the order would be filled and packed. The salesman would receive a fifteen percent commission, and then the accounts receivable people would do the follow-through to get the invoice paid, and so forth. There was a lot of procedure and built-in cost that would invariably drive up the price of the item, so we were never much interested in this approach. As I've indicated, our profit pie simply wasn't big enough to cut into so many pieces.

Still, there was an entire segment of customers we weren't reaching in any kind of orchestrated way—people who only purchased their hair care items directly from their salons or stylists. So we remained open to any new ways to tap that market. And it wasn't just the salon customers who represented big sales, but the salons themselves; they used a considerable amount of shampoos and dying and styling products in their own shops, all of which translated into potential sales. With this in mind, then, one of our people tipped me off to a small chain of beauty supply stores operating in the southern states known as Sally Beauty Supply. The tip came from a lifelong friend of mine named Dan Lewis, who headed our professional products division; he came on board after having success in other arenas and quickly emerged as one of our top people. The concept was simple: the Sally stores were closed to the general public, but salon owners and other beauty professionals could shop there and buy directly off the shelves, thereby eliminating a lot of the cost involved for the wholesaler. There were ten Sally stores at the time, one of them company-owned in New Orleans. The rest of them were franchised. After examining their operations, we determined that they were actually quite profitable. Or, I should say, potentially profitable. They weren't being especially well run, and we felt we could do a better job, so we came in with an offer to buy the company. It was essentially a stock-swap sort of deal, and it made sense for us for the opportunity it offered.

Our first order of business with this new company was to change over to a system of all corporate-owned stores because our feeling was that we'd never get the stores in line unless we managed them directly. Next, we looked to expand our base and open several new stores under the Sally name. We did this first in the South, where the name had some currency among area beauticians, but the game plan was to move north and west at first opportunity. (At this writing, we own and operate more than twenty-three hundred Sally Beauty Supply stores all over the world, so, clearly, we expanded the heck out of this thing.)

The most strategically sound move regarding Sally, however, was the decision to install Mike Renzulli as head of this new division. He came from a background in the pharmaceutical industry. Specifically, he worked in his father's drugstore, but he was a talented young go-getter looking for a place to make his mark. Happily, this niche presented by the Sally acquisition was a good fit. I looked to Renzulli because he reminded me a little bit of myself; he was a tireless self-starter driven to succeed. He actually corresponded with me for a number of years before we even met. He sent letters from his home in Philadelphia, offering quite reasonable ideas or suggestions about our products.

Really, some of his insights were remarkable, and I thought that they had a lot of merit. One day, out of the blue, my secretary came in to tell me there was a Mr. Renzulli to see me. He drove out to Chicago with his wife and two small children and came to the office without an appointment, hoping for an opportunity. I was happy to give him one. Really, he was quite an impressive young fellow. I couldn't offer him the kind of money he made in his father's business, but I put him in the marketing department. He had done very well in a short space of time when this Sally opportunity rolled around.

As it turned out, the association wasn't as win-win as this simple math suggested. We had a successful line of professional products sold to salons through wholesale brokers. Our move into Sally threatened to take customers from some of those same wholesalers, who, before long, stopped doing business with us altogether as we started opening up more and more stores, thereby stepping on their market share. It was the classic case of one hand not knowing what the other was doing, in terms of our internal culture at Alberto-Culver. Our Sally stores were growing, and, of course, Mike Renzulli and his people didn't much care if they were cutting into the business of their competitors because those were essentially their marching orders. But our professional division began to feel the pinch of that success. That division was having a good deal of trouble moving our lines through traditional wholesaling channels; other wholesalers wouldn't carry our products, so revenues from that one division began to fall off. I chose to take the long view and let the professional division suffer while we expanded the Sally outfit on the theory that, in success, the Sally franchise would far outpace the losses we suffered at the hands of the disgruntled wholesalers. And, in the end, this proved to be the prudent course, but those "growing pains" years were difficult on our various bottom lines.

Another fallout from the success of our Sally stores was the too-common industry practice of "diverting"—that is, the unethical selling by wholesalers into the retail markets. Some unscrupulous merchandisers realized early on that they could buy our items in bulk on a wholesale basis, then undercut our pricing with grocery and drug store chains. At that time, in fact, personal hair care items weren't typically sold in grocery stores; the shelf space came available through these diverted sales, which, of course, infuriated the buyers at Walgreen's, Thrifty's, and other drug and discount chains where we spent years developing relationships. It was a tremendous problem, and the only way I could see to combat it was with our flagship brand—the VO5 hairdressing. This was possibly one of the most difficult decisions I ever had to make as the head of this company, but there was no way to keep our margins intact in the face of such rampant diverting without cutting off all sales of Alberto VO5 to professional outlets. In this way, I kept the main buyers happy, and since these were the chains that built our brands in the first place, I felt I had no choice. If our Sally customers wanted to divert the bulk purchases of our competitors, I didn't much mind, but I wouldn't have them underselling our bread-and-butter partners from the drug and discount chains on our own merchandise.

From that moment on, virtually every wholesaler and beauty salon owner wanted nothing to do with Alberto-Culver products. Our Alberto VO5 line had represented a nice source of income for them, but I couldn't abide these diverting tactics. I had to protect our core business, even if it cost us a substantial secondary business. Unavoidably, the impact of that decision is still felt in our vast network of Sally stores, where you can no longer find Alberto-Culver products. We do sell the VO5 hairdressing in a targeted few stores in Florida for reasons that I won't go into here, but, across the board, we carry only our competitors' lines. We've become the single largest customer for L'Oréal and for Revlon.

It's an unlikely setup, don't you think? Personally, I've never heard of anything like it—a manufacturer selling and creating its own brands and marketing them worldwide, and, at the same time, participating in the success of its principal competitors—but it's been a real boost to our earnings. The Sally stores currently account for more than 50 percent of our total revenues, and it all started from that one store we kept open in New Orleans and our willingness to make tough, short-term decisions in order to achieve our long-range goals.

⌐⳽⳾⳽⳾⳽⳾⌐

Are you familiar with the old adage, the more things change the more they stay the same? Well, in my professional experience at least, that's a load of hogwash. We set up shop during a time of enormous change—in terms of communication, travel, manufacturing, marketing, technology, and on and on—and with each transformation, it was as if we no longer could recognize the landscape we left behind. We would do things in certain ways for certain periods, and then we'd look up and realize that those ways were out of date.

Consider, for example, the sweeping changes television brought to our culture and the changes, in turn, our culture brought back to television. They went hand in hand. In 1955, when we were just starting out, the penetration into American homes was nothing like it became by the end of the 1960s. As a marketing tool, the medium had not yet hit its stride, and it was possible to purchase commercial time on our shoestring budget. Over time, however, advertising rates soared to match the number of people tuning in, and the production values in certain types of commercials also rose as viewers became accustomed to being entertained by these ads. We reached a point where we could no longer afford to blanket the airwaves with the kind of frequency we all felt our products needed to make an impact on sales, and we found ourselves in an ironic, Catch-22 situation: we were now a deep-pocketed, publicly traded, wildly successful company, but even we couldn't afford the advertising rates being charged by the major networks for their top shows.

Of course, we needed television to move our products, so what did we do? Well, we looked to reinvent the wheel a little bit—or at least to grease it. In those days, the standard practice in the television industry was to run sixty-second commercials. I don't know who came up with that format in the first place, but it was the order of the day, and it had been for some time. The trouble was, with the skyrocketing rates, we couldn't afford to buy time with the frequency we felt we needed to turn our household products into household names. The easy answer, we believed, was to produce shorter commercials—say, thirty-seconds instead of sixty. To this end, we did a number of tests to see if we could be just as persuasive in communicating our message and selling our products in these shorter spots. We worked closely with Horace Schwerin, who was, at that time, the guru of testing in the advertising community. We determined that yes, indeed, we could make the same impact on consumers with a thirty-second pitch as we could with a sixty-second pitch.

The next hurdle came in acting on these results. We looked first to buy the standard sixty-second slots and fill them with two thirty-second commercials run back to back to advertise for two products instead of one. In this way, we felt that we could effectively double the value of our media buy. But it wasn't so simple. The networks didn't like that we were going against the grain in this way, and even the independent stations didn't like it, so the buys were turned down. Then, as now, an advertiser had to submit his commercial for review before it could get on the air. We went to all the trouble and expense of producing two thirty-second spots, testing them to determine their effectiveness, and we couldn't get them on the air. Let me tell you, it was enormously frustrating, and yet I didn't think that I could do anything with this frustration except to set it aside. Sometimes, you have no choice but to accept the status quo, and, at first, I determined that this was one of those times. However, in talking to our outside legal counsel, Ted Laughlin, on another matter, I happened to vent on this advertising impasse. Laughlin suggested that I let him look into the matter on our behalf. He had been an antitrust attorney with the government before moving into private practice, and he felt that there might be something to our position.

Well, several days later, Laughlin came back with his opinion that we could likely make a case against the networks or the independent station owners for rejecting our back-to-back ads. He said that we could make a claim on our own or solicit support from a group of advertisers, and he suggested that if we prevailed, we'd be entitled to a great sum of money. I thought this was interesting, but I wasn't prepared to start a lawsuit. It made no sense to irritate people with whom we had to continue to do business because even if the claim was allowed, we'd be worse off in the end. Nevertheless, I felt emboldened by the lawyer's findings, enough so that I managed to persuade a single independent station owner to carry our back-to-back thirty-second spots. And from there, I managed to persuade another. And another. All with extremely positive results, I might add. We saw the same bump in sales we saw with traditional sixty-second spots in the days immediately following each airing.

The networks were a tougher sell. The objection of the network brass was never fully articulated, but I always suspected that it was out of fear. They were afraid that if our thirty-second spots proved popular and effective, advertisers would clamor for these shorter commercials, and the networks somehow would lose money. They wanted to protect their franchise, which certainly was understandable. Shortsighted, but understandable.

I was very public about our efforts to shake up standard commercial length and very public about the networks' unwillingness to put our shorter spots on the air. Word of these doings reached the National Association of Broadcasters, a high-minded group of industry heavyweights who gathered each year to discuss matters of shared importance and, of course, to stretch the parameters of their expense accounts at the group's annual conventions. In any event, the NAB graciously invited me to speak to the trade on the matter. I happily accepted, thinking this might open a dialogue on the issue and get things moving toward a positive resolution.

Alberto-Culver was one of the leading television advertisers at the time. Readers old enough undoubtedly will recall our spots for SugarTwin sugar substitute, Kleen Guard furniture polish, New Dawn hair coloring, and Alberto VO5 shampoo, in addition to our flagship brands. We were a fairly ubiquitous presence on the television scene. As a result, I guess my voice carried a lot of weight in the advertising and broadcasting communities, and I thought it prudent to share the spotlight with the attorney, Ted Laughlin. He was an expert in matters of antitrust, and it seemed to me that a scholarly opinion on whether or not advertisers should be free to produce commercials of any length would be far more meaningful than my own gut instinct or my hard-won sense of right and wrong. To me, it was a no-brainer: let the networks and the independent station owners determine how they wanted to sell their available advertising time, and let the advertisers decide how they wanted to fill it. But I didn't want my opinion dismissed as naïve or pie-in-the-sky, so I brought in reinforcements.

I began my presentation by discussing how essential television was to the growth of our company, and I spoke generally about the reliance of all consumer products on the mass advertising opportunities the medium offered. Then I announced what most everyone in the auditorium already knew, that we had been experimenting with thirty-second commercials and were hoping to have a chance to place them on the air. Then I introduced Ted Laughlin, and he went off on so many powerfully persuasive antitrust tangents backed by case law that he soon had half the people in the room scratching their heads and the other half nodding in agreement. The upshot of his talk, though, was that it got the network people thinking. It got them thinking that there was indeed demand for this type of advertising, and they would do well to embrace it. After all, they could sell these half-minute spots for slightly more than 50 percent of the full-minute rates, so, in the long run, they would come out ahead if they sold through their available time.

Before I even left the luncheon, one network representative assured me that I could run our back-to-back commercials on his air, and another indicated that he was willing to do the same once he cleared the matter with his colleagues. This, many industry analysts now believe, was the beginning of the end of the sixty-second commercial. Nowadays, you hardly ever see a sixty-second spot, except on special event programs like the Super Bowl. Little by little, the thirty-second commercial became the standard, and if you go back to the Museum of Broadcasting now and view some of those famous old commercials, you'll notice that the sixty-second spots tend to drag. The pace has changed, and we have changed with it. At first, advertising agencies didn't like the shorter canvas. They felt that they needed the time to tell a story, to paint a picture, to create brand awareness and loyalty. But that, too, was a lot of hogwash. (They also felt, foolishly, that the production costs would decrease, without realizing there would be a windfall of additional spots to more than make up the difference.) With practice, creative advertisers learned to telegraph their message and to make an even more effective pitch. It was just a matter of working within the parameters they were given. It's worth noting that a decade or so later, advertisers, led again by Alberto-Culver, tinkered with fifteen-second spots, which today have become something of a standard.

During the mid 1960s and early 1970s, Alberto-Culver had a reputation for being a very aggressive buyer of commercial television time, but we were also known for buying "better" than our competitors. That is, we sought out new, controversial, talked-about programs; we weren't content to pay top dollar for a top-rated show that may have been watched by millions of people unlikely to need our products. We went to stations with creative deals that allowed us to buy up time at sixty or seventy cents on the dollar. For example, we bought time in bulk, which, in those days, was not the common practice it has become. If an outlet asked for ten thousand dollars per minute, we offered eight thousand with a promise to buy more minutes. We were able to strike a series of favorable deals—favorable to both parties, in fact.

Advertising agencies were just beginning to look at things like demographics, the kind of orchestrated media buying that targets specific viewers by age and gender and is tailored to the product or service sold. I wasn't a big fan of such targeting early on. I used to tell our advertising people when they came to me to explain that a smart demographic buy was like a rifle shot precisely aimed at a specific target that I'd much rather have buck shot. In many respects, I still feel the same way. Give me the widest possible audience at the most reasonable cost per viewer, and I'll build an effective advertising campaign.

Over the years, I developed a reputation as being something of a television nut, meaning I would only advertise on television. That was never the case, although it was true that our television spending outstripped our print spending by a significant margin, primarily because it cost so much more to advertise on television than it did anywhere else. But there's no denying that print works on a slower timetable. The conventional wisdom in our office is that you need to make seven impressions in a print ad before you can persuade someone to go out and buy your product. So, that takes time. You can make those seven impressions in consecutive issues of the same magazine, but if you're dealing with a monthly, that can take more than half a year.

Back to television. We tended to cut against the norm. When everyone was making spot buys, we made big opportunity purchases. When the trend shifted to up-front buying, we looked to pick our spots. These days, most major advertisers purchase their prime time network advertising up front, during the spring purchasing season, but I always tell our people to limit, to some extent, that kind of buying. Why? Well, for one thing, you're buying untested shows. You don't know what the popular new shows are going to be. You may have some ideas, but you don't know. If all new shows were guaranteed winners, they'd all pull precisely the same audience, week in and week out. Plus, there's always an objection or two lodged by some religious or special interest group over the contents of one show or another, and I never wanted to be locked in as the sponsor of that one controversial show. So our strategy at Alberto-Culver became to keep more than 50 percent of our advertising budget in reserve because it often happened that, at the last minute, there was an opening on an established hit that the network needed to fill. I can't tell you how many times we shared space on the same program with, say, Sears Roebuck, where the up-front advertiser paid much more than we did.

We have our own phrase for this type of media-buying, in house. We call it "opportunistic" buying, and the theory behind it goes back to the impulse to split those customer sixty-second commercials in half all those years ago. Why pay full value, or what someone perceives to be full value, when there are sound, innovative ways to pay less? It makes no sense to me, for example, to over-pay for a spot on a high-profile event like the Academy Awards when I can stretch the same money much farther by making some of these logical, value-based buys. And, it made no sense to continue to pay for a sixty-second commercial when our instincts and our research agreed that a thirty-second commercial would achieve the same result.

Innovation pays, wouldn't you agree?

<hr />

In its first full decade, the Alberto-Culver Company exceeded beyond my wildest expectations. Goodness, it even eclipsed my wildest dreams. We developed a number of successful new products, created and now dominated a number of new product categories, and stood quite prominently as one of the leading and most innovative advertisers on television. We employed more than two thousand people, enjoyed annuals sales exceeding one hundred million dollars, sold our products in more than fifty countries, and, in almost every respect, stood poised to achieve even greater success in the decade ahead.

For a publicly traded company such as ours, such quick-out-of-the-gate success can sometimes be a mixed blessing. I was always careful to keep the company a very closely held concern. It was anathema to me, the thought that some corporate raider might swoop in and buy Alberto-Culver right out from under us after Bernice and I sweated out those early years and guided the early growth. Indeed, throughout the late 1960s and into the early 1970s, there were a great many high-profile hostile takeovers in such industries as entertainment, consumer goods, manufacturing, transportation, and so forth. No sector was immune to the phenomenon, and, privately, I worried that the more successful we became, the more attractive we made ourselves to a corporate raider. Of course, at the same time, I also worried that despite our long list of positives, perhaps we weren't appealing to an outside investor, and this was the flip-side to the runaway growth dilemma. Simple pragmatism said to avoid being a target, while simple vanity would have left me feeling secretly insulted if we weren't on somebody's wish-list.

Of course, I had no intention of seeing the company wrested from my control, which was why, in our public offering, we only made a small percentage of stock available to the general public. Bernice and I controlled approximately 40 percent of all outstanding shares personally, and there was another 15 or 20 percent held by our close friends and associates, people like McCabe, Stone, and Arrington. Our by-laws were written in such a way that mandated 75 percent of the vote on matters such as a change in management, so even with just our 40 percent we had it covered. We were, I felt, fairly well insulated from the takeover winds blowing through the markets during this period, which was why I was able to approach the few tentative advances on our turf with a certain level of bemusement. I chose to be flattered by them, instead of threatened.

One such overture stands out. In 1966, the conglomerate Gulf and Western took over the world-famous Paramount Studios and, in the bargain, signaled an all-bets-are-off raid on certain icons of American industry. (Indeed, the company's reputation as a corporate raider became so entrenched in the culture that the comedian Mel Brooks referred to it as "Engulf and Devour.") Charles Bludhorn, the fiery chairman of Gulf and Western, who spoke in a fantastically rich German-Austrian accent, was soon enough the very symbol of the corporate takeover, which was why my heart raced a bit when my secretary told me he was on the line, hoping to speak to me. The man was legendary for his corporate buying sprees or, I should say, his acquisitive nature.

I picked up the phone right away. "Hello, Mr. Bludhorn," I said, more cheerfully than the situation perhaps warranted. "What can I do for you?" I felt for just a moment like the young co-ed finally being asked to a dance she never really wanted to attend.

"Leonard," he said, dispensing with the formalities, "I just wanted you to know that today I purchased one hundred thousand shares of Alberto-Culver stock."

"That's great, Mr. Bludhorn," I said, not knowing what else to offer, but wanting to keep the conversation going a while longer. "Tell me, what are planning to do with it?"

"I plan to be one of your principal investors," he said. "I didn't want someone else coming and taking over." He started to feed me a line about how we Americans should stick together in matters such as these, how you never could be too careful in the current business environment, how he merely had my company's interests at heart, and so on and so forth. I chose to listen politely until he was through.

"Well, Mr. Bludhorn," I said, when he'd spoken his piece, "we're glad to have you aboard."

One hundred thousand shares, at that time, gave Charlie Bludhorn a significant stake in our company, but not so significant that it amounted to anything in terms of a voting bloc. However, a few days later, he called me back, and I could only guess what was coming.

"Hello, Charlie," I said. "Good to hear from you." In truth, it was and it wasn't. I was flattered at his continued interest in Alberto-Culver and took it as a kind of back-handed compliment, but, at the same time, I didn't want to be too flattered, if you know what I mean. The first block of shares was enough of a compliment, thank you very much.

"Leonard," he said, "I want you to know that today I purchased another two hundred fifty thousand shares of Alberto stock."

I said, "That's fantastic, Charlie. You must really like what we're doing to take such a strong position."

At that point, Charlie Bludhorn was a long way away from amassing the kind of stake in our company that would cause me any real worry.

Well, I took another phone call or two from my new friend Charlie, another hundred thousand shares here, another fifty thousand shares there, and when his position exceeded half of a million shares, I gave it to him straight. "Charlie," I said, "I consider all these purchases a tremendous show of support, but I can't help thinking you've got something else in mind. Let me assure you, I'm extremely happy you're on board, but I want you to know what I control." Then I told him about the type of support I believed I had from other large stockholders who, together with Bernice and me, have 65 percent of the voting shares.

The phone went dead. For the longest time, Charlie Bludhorn didn't say a word. It was, perhaps, the longest stretch of time in the man's loud and demonstrative career that he was tongue-tied. Finally, he thanked me for my candor and bid me goodbye. Eventually we bought back the stock at a discount to what he had paid.

I never heard from him again. In the silence, I found an important message: you can't always get what you want in business, as elsewhere, but if you're careful, intelligent, and possibly even a little bit prescient, you can very often keep what you've earned.

# 8

---

# Horse Sense

As a child, I went to the racetrack constantly, but, unlike most Chicago youths, I did so with the blessing (and, frequently, the aiding and abetting) of my father. See, the horses were a great passion in our household, as I have written, and the very first Kentucky Derby I had the pleasure of seeing left its mark. Oh, that Run for the Roses was a beauty! It was 1928, and my entire family went to Churchill Downs as the guests of my father's friend, John Hertz. The weather was lousy, as I recall, but what did a nine-year-old boy care about the weather?

Mr. Hertz was, at that time, the owner of the Yellow Cab Company in Chicago, which he later quite famously parlayed into a car rental business under his name. He was also a fairly successful breeder of thoroughbred racehorses and a prominent figure in the racing community, so it was a special honor to take in the Derby in his company and in his high style. (Really, to a small boy, such grandeur was very nearly sinful!) Also special was the winning performance of Reigh Count, a legendary horse who became one of the great stud horses of all time—he sired Count Fleet, who won the Triple Crown. The raw excitement of that race, with all those champion horses hurtling and splashing through the mud in pursuit of excellence has been with me ever after. In some ways, every race I've seen since has paled by comparison, and yet each one holds the promise of another just like it before the gate opens and those proud, glorious horses take flight.

From that moment forward, you couldn't keep my father and me from Arlington Park in Chicago, where, during the season, we were something like regulars. And you couldn't keep us from the Derby, either. For this, the entire family turned out. Every year, we turned it into a special trip unless, of course, some real-world concerns got in our way. I couldn't wager, of course, but I could root for my father's picks to come in the money. I confess here that very often the thrill was not in the betting, but in the pageantry and splendor of the race and the fine trappings of the sport. And, if the Kentucky Derby was our World Series, then a day at Arlington was like a regular season game at Wrigley Field, where I cheered for my beloved Cubs. But in at least one respect, it was on a level all its own. For those few minutes during each race, there was nothing to match the surge of power and rush of adrenaline as the splendid animals raced toward the finish line. The runaway enthusiasm of the fans. The fierce, striving beauty. The shared sense of hope and anticipation. And the sheer possibility of cheering on a winner.

My father was the sort of man who made the acquaintance of a great many people from all walks of life. It so happened that he was also friendly with the fellow who owned Arlington Park, a man named Ben Lindheimer, who was a major force in thoroughbred racing for many, many years. In those days, attendance at many of the more prominent racetracks around the country was soaring, although, in some regions, the gate was adversely affected by the depressing economic climate, and some tracks were forced to close. But Arlington remained a top draw throughout most of the Depression. I spent countless afternoons in the grandstand rooting for my favorite jockeys, learning how to read the racing form and how to handicap, understanding the habits of certain trainers, and generally studying the ins and outs of the horse business. Sometimes, we sat in one of the boxes with my father's well-heeled friends, but, most of the time, we sat by ourselves in general admission. Happily, my "once-removed" friendship with Mr. Lindheimer gave me a little more access to the track than most kids my age, and I was sure to take full advantage. After all, I'd learned my lesson well: if I was ever going to bet on a situation out of my direct control, I would do so only after learning as much as I possibly could about the likely outcome.

But they wouldn't call it gambling if there was such a thing as a sure bet, right? Predictably, my youthful swagger took me headlong into my first disappointment as a betting man, although it wasn't that big a disappointment, and I was hardly a man. I never bet on the horses when I was with my father, but, being a hard-nosed Depression-era kid, I often found ways to wager on my own. In those days, everybody in the neighborhood took bets: the druggist, the barber, the corner grocer, local bookies of various types. You couldn't cross a downtown street without bumping into a bookie. You weren't supposed to bet if you were underage, but, by the time, I reached high school, I usually could slip a fifty-cent wager past even the most vigilant neighborhood soul. And I did, often with good success, but just as often with no positive result. This, I learned, was a part of the game, and I was careful never to bet more money than I could afford to lose. Of course, I had no real money at all during much of the 1930s, certainly nothing I could fritter away on chance. But I found reasons to justify a small wager here and there, and I was enough of a handicapper to come out mostly ahead.

I wrote earlier about the commission house my uncle ran during the Depression, and his association with all these high rollers and Chicago sportsmen eventually led him and my father to a rare opportunity. They bought a horse. Or, perhaps, they bought a share of a horse—enough of a share that they had a voice in how he was trained, how he was raced, and so forth. I never learned all the details of their ownership arrangement, and what I did know, I found out about quite by accident. One Friday night, my aunt and uncle came over to the house for Sabbath dinner. In those days, my mother used to cook up a traditional Jewish meal on Friday nights: chicken soup, gefilte fish, roast chicken. We weren't especially religious, but we were traditional; it got to the point where we ate so much chicken soup that I never touched the stuff once I left the house. (I still avoid it, when I can.)

My aunt and uncle were frequent guests at these Friday night dinners, but, on this one evening, I asked to be excused from the table before dessert. As I moved from the dining room table, I overheard a hushed conversation between my father and my uncle that wasn't meant for me. My father had a small library just off the living room, where he used to read and conduct business, and, through the door, I got the kind of earful that sends young hearts soaring. They were talking about their horse—it was not quite two years old and really could run. I thought, a horse! *Our* horse! The idea that we Lavins were suddenly horse people sent a chill through my adolescent bones. Naturally, I let my mind race to a trip to the winner's circle at the Kentucky Derby, and it was a grand, sweet dream.

Inevitably, the bulletin about owning the horse came with a scheme. It was my father's scheme first, and my uncle's, but I latched onto it with one of my own. It wouldn't do to tell my father and uncle that I had overheard their conversation, but, at the same time, it wouldn't do to let the news it contained go unnoticed. Apparently, their plan with the horse was to hold him back in his first three races, not to let anybody know his true abilities, and then to make a killing in the fourth race, when the odds were long against them.

The horse's name was Shama Thrush, and it sounded so exotic and promising that I couldn't wait to tell my two best friends: Dan Lewis, who some years later joined the Alberto-Culver Company to head our professional division, and Fred Rosati. I laid it out for them as accurately as I could, and soon it was agreed that the three of us would pool our nickels and dimes and wait for our opportunity to put the pot on Shama Thrush in his fourth race. He was still a yearling, so he wasn't racing just yet, but his debut would come soon enough. In the weeks and months ahead, we lived on a kids' version of an austerity budget. We did without ice cream, picture shows, and virtually every other treat our meager allowances previously allowed. As I recall, we each received about ten cents a week from our parents, and we were diligent about saving it. When the time was right and our pool overflowing, we'd bet it all on Shama Thrush and clean up. There were bookies on every corner in a city like Chicago, and even though we were underage, we wouldn't have any trouble passing off a series of small wagers, particularly in parts of town where we weren't well known. Goodness, if our parents had any idea what we were scheming, they would have strung us up!

The waiting seemed to stretch on for ages, but, in the waiting, we amassed a sizeable stake of about twenty-five dollars, which, when I think back on it, was a tremendous sum. We followed Shama Thrush in the newspapers. There were no off-track betting parlors or other means to track a race in real time, but, each morning, we read the sports pages to see which horses were running out at Arlington. I also picked up snippets of information on the horse from my father, who was happy to talk to me about a subject of such mutual interest. In his own way, he confirmed what I overheard that Friday night, that they would ease the horse onto the circuit quietly and hold him back in his first few races before seeing what he could do. He said this with more of a sporting interest than a betting interest, but I had enough horse sense to read between the lines.

Finally, Shama Thrush turned up in the betting line, and I was so excited I couldn't wait to run down to the corner to tell my friends, but, as it turned out, we were all on the same page. They'd spotted it, too. The comment from the handicapper was that the horse was a first-timer and was expected to run decently, but not to be a factor at the finish. Sure enough, the horse went off at about eight to one odds and finished at the butt end of the middle of the pack. Certainly, an unspectacular debut, which was exactly what my father and my uncle wanted.

Three weeks later, the routine was much the same. The hand-icapper hadn't seen anything to recommend the horse during its first time out, and so Shama Thrush went off at even longer odds, about fifteen to one. This time, he finished even farther back in the pack.

By the third time, we all knew the drill, and Shama Thrush ran at even longer odds to an even poorer showing.

Finally, the day of his fourth race arrived, and we three mus-keteers were ready to burst with excitement. Our savings had reached that unthinkable total of twenty-five dollars, and we had worked out a plan to get some of the older neighborhood boys to place our bets for us all over town. We offered them 10 percent of our winnings to put down two dollars with the barber, the gro-cer, the druggist, and so on. We could have placed the bets our-selves, but we didn't want to raise any eyebrows. Plus, with all that money on a single, no-account horse, we thought most bookies would be unlikely to take the bet.

It was a school day, as I recall, and, as we sat in school, it start-ed to rain. And it wasn't just any rain. It was a regular downpour. I looked out the window and wondered what the rain might mean to our winnings. I wasn't sophisticated enough to know whether a horse that runs well on a dry track can also run well in the mud, but even if I'd had some ideas, it was too late. Our bets were in place.

As it happened, my father and my uncle also weren't too sure how Shama Thrush would handle the mud, and they weren't about to find out. They'd already agreed that if the fourth race turned up wet, they'd hold him back for another outing and clean up on the fifth race. The problem for me and Dan Lewis and Fred Rosati was that I didn't happen to overhear this part of the con-versation, so our money went down the drain. If memory serves, I think our horse finished dead last.

So much for our grand scheme.

On Shama Thush's fifth outing, just to put a capper on the story, the horse ran true to form and shocked the field. Largely due to those lackluster performances in his first four races, he went off at extremely long odds—forty-five to one, or thereabouts—and my father and my uncle made an absolute killing. Surely, they put more than twenty-five dollars on the race, but even capped by our initial stake, we three friends would have done fabulously well.

At this point, though, after losing all our money on Shama Thrush's previous outing, we didn't have a penny among us, so we had to sit this one out. Even as there was great joy in our household for the surprising good fortune of this surprising young horse, I allowed myself to despair.

But I got over it soon enough. The disappointment over Shama Thrush didn't dampen my zest for the sport, and, throughout my childhood, the majesty and wonder of the horse races stood as a good and wonderful thing. None of us had very much money in those days, but at the racetrack, for a few hours, my father and I could move about like kings and princes and soak in the rarified air of some of the great sportsmen, industrialists, and headline-makers of the day.

And so, my education at the hands of some of the leading lights of the thoroughbred industry proceeded apace, and, in the process, my enthusiasm for the so-called "sport of kings" never abated. If anything, it grew. It grew to the point that, as a young Navy man, I spent virtually all of my free time at Laurel Race Track in Maryland after the Navy transferred me to the East Coast. And it grew to the point that, as a young married man, I looked to share that passion with my young wife, Bernice. Bernice—bless her spirited soul!—took to it with great, good cheer.

And, as our efforts with the Alberto-Culver Corporation began to pay dividends, I returned to the track with even greater fervor. My own circle of friends began to match my father's, and I once again traveled in high style among some of the more prosperous denizens of the world of sports. I don't set this out to brag, but accurately to portray how it was to have grown up in the company of the sport's elite and to return once again to these circles through my various business associations.

It was on one such outing, in the company of my good friend Ted Doyle and his lovely wife, Charlotte, that my lifelong love affair with the thoroughbreds took a turn toward the professional. Ted had been the publisher of the *Herald-American* in New York and the *Chicago American* in Chicago, and he had since come to work for us as our director of communications. For some reason, that Saturday afternoon was running pretty much to form, at least according to the way I had handicapped each race. I picked winner after winner, and a lot of my other prognostications—such as which horses didn't stand a chance, and so forth—also came to pass. At one point, Doyle leaned over to me and said, "Leonard, I've been to the races many times, but I've never sat with someone so knowledgeable. You really know your stuff, and you seem to love it. Have you ever thought about going into the thoroughbred business?"

Quite frankly, it had never even occurred to me to turn this lifelong passion into an avocation of some kind, but once Ted put the thought out there, I could think of little else. I went home and talked it over with Bernice, and we agreed that it might be something to pursue as a sideline. I must admit, I found the prospect terribly exciting, and I couldn't wait to call Ted the next morning to tell him he'd given me the push for which I didn't even know I was waiting.

As it turned out, Ted was on friendly terms with the general manager of the *Daily Racing Form* in Chicago, a man named Mel Shrier, and he put the two of us in touch. I told Shrier about my newly hatched ambition to run my own stable, and it seemed to me the most prudent course was to find a trainer before I went looking for any horses at auction. The horses would come and go, I knew, but a smart, dependable, intuitive trainer would serve my operation well for many years to come. Shrier directed me to two big-time freelance trainers, and I flew them both in to Chicago for interviews. I was quite impressed with a tall Texan by the name of Willard Proctor, and I offered him the job.

Willard Proctor's first order of business was to get us some horses. I went with him to a few auctions, and we looked for a horse that had established itself and still could race. It's not always an easy order to fill because when a horse is up for sale, there's often some mitigating reason for it. But there are always trainers who believe a certain horse was mishandled by another stable and so forth, so there are bound to be buying opportunities.

A couple weeks later, Willard called and told me he found a mare that seemed to be sound—and a sound investment. Her name was Gabby Abby, and she set me back seventy-five thousand dollars, which, in 1965, was a good deal of money to speculate on a horse. I didn't have a budget or an overall plan of attack. I just figured we would take this thing day by day. If there was a horse with which we felt we could do something on the circuit or out to stud, then I would consider the cost on a case-by-case basis. Meanwhile, I was anxious to get into the winner's circle, so I let Willard Proctor convince me that Gabby Abby would take me there. And sure enough he was right. He was right about a lot of things, which I suppose was why I hired him.

That mare's very first race was a gem. We entered her out at Arlington Park, and I've got to admit I was fairly nonchalant about this new enterprise. When it came time to register the horse with the track stewards, I had to give them a name for our stable. I didn't want to run Gabby Abby under my own name or under the company name because Alberto-Culver was now a public company, and I didn't want it to appear that I was some spendthrift, squandering a stock market windfall on the horses. So Bernice and I scratched our heads to come up with a name. Every good name we came up with was taken or otherwise unsuitable, and it wasn't until race day that we came upon a winner. We'd really been stymied by this one because, of course, we wanted to come up with a name that would serve us well for many years. We all expected to be at this business a good long time, so this was no casual christening.

On the way to the track, we passed a billboard advertising a new real estate development called the Glen Hill Townhouses. I turned to Bernice and said, "That's our name. Glen Hill Farms. Do you like it?"

She said that it was all right with her, and we were in business.

Of course, we needed to race under our own colors, but we already anticipated that. I asked our art department to come up with something patterned after our Alberto VO5 hairdressing tube, which we all thought would be rather distinctive: orange, black, and gold. No one was racing under those colors, so we had some silks made up, and we were ready to go.

Before the race, I bet two hundred dollars on Gabby Abby for the jockey, as a kind of incentive. I thought it would help him to win, and I actually walked down to the paddock to hand the fellow the ticket. Proctor looked at me like I was an idiot, which I imagine I was. To bet on your own horse was, of course, quite common, and to bet on behalf of your jockey was also quite common, but, apparently, it was a *faux pas* to hand the ticket over to the jockey while he was up on the horse. I just shrugged and thought, oh, well, what do I know?

In any event, the gambit must have worked, *faux pas* or no, because Gabby Abby crossed the wire ahead of the field, and we were all very excited. The whole family was out at the track with us that day, and we all went down to the winner's circle and posed for pictures and so forth. It was a wonderful, spirited moment— the first of many, we all hoped.

⁂

To his friends, Willard Proctor was known as Prock. I'm proud to say that before too terribly long, he counted me in this group, but I'm prouder still that our friendship lasted more than forty years. And, as our friendship grew, so did Glen Hill Farms. Naturally, we couldn't build a stable on the back of one horse alone, so we hit the road in search of bargains. In the thoroughbred business, as in other endeavors, you did well to hedge your bets; no owner worth his feed would throw all his resources after just one animal. Prock was of the opinion that none of the yearlings offered at auction at Saratoga in upstate New York or at the Keeneland sales in Kentucky were worth a penny over thirty thousand dollars, and I was inclined to agree. Of course, some of the horses fetched sums far greater than Prock's assessment, but we tried never to eclipse that mark. On those occasions when we came in substantially under that figure, we counted ourselves lucky. Nowadays, comparable horses routinely sell for more than one million dollars, but Prock was a very conservative man—particularly when he spent someone else's money. He was also an inordinately honest man, as I subsequently discovered, and someone on whom I came to rely a great deal as we moved forward in this shared enterprise.

Two yearling fillies from the Saratoga sale soon joined Gabby Abby in our stable, although, at this early stage, to call our small, new business a "stable" was perhaps a stretch of the imagination. Glen Hill Farms was a "farm" in name only, without even a barn to call our own. We actually had to go looking for a place to keep the two yearlings until they could be broken and trained, while Gabby Abby, as an established horse, was quartered elsewhere. Each time we purchased a new horse, we had to make separate arrangements for training, stabling, and so forth.

Early on, Prock continued to train and acquire horses for other owners. In fact, when I found him he was training for a legendary thoroughbred figure named Arthur "Bull" Hancock, who ran Clairborne Farms in Lexington, Kentucky, the biggest and most prestigious racing farm in the country. He worked for other owners, too; his services were much in demand. Soon, though, I managed to convince Prock to throw in exclusively with Glen Hill Farms, and it was a happy, successful association for many years, until his death just a few years ago. During that time, the operation of Glen Hill Farms became a regular family affair for the

Proctors. Prock's brother Alan became my farm manager, and he has been succeeded by Prock's son Hap—short for Harry A. Proctor. And Prock's son Tom is now my trainer, so clearly the partnership between the Lavin and Proctor families has been a profitable one for all concerned.

And speaking of profit, our farm ran at one almost immediately—on a small scale at first, to be sure, but a profitable small scale. Prock was a good and sensible manager of our fortunes, and he never bought a horse unless he felt it might bring us a sensible return on a reasonable timetable. We bought horses, ran them to some measure of success in races around the country, entered them in claiming races, and, with good showings, sold them for handsome profits.

Eventually, as we started to grow, Prock and I determined that we also would breed horses, which I'd quickly learned was a key component to any successful thoroughbred operation and, perhaps, the most gratifying. To me, the prospect of breeding a strong horse and winning a big race with it was the ultimate goal, and I realized that we needed to have our own farm to accomplish it. It would no longer do to lease space in other stables, to have our horses stationed throughout the country. It made no sense economically, and it made no sense as a practical matter, as well. If your plan is to own just a few horses, then such an arrangement makes perfect sense, but our plans quickly ran to something much bigger. We needed to centralize our operation, and the only way to do this was on our own land. We had good horses by the middle 1960s, top horses winning top races, but I felt that we never would reach the next level unless we had a farm to call our own. So Prock and I set about looking for suitable acreage in a suitable climate at a suitable price. Lexington, Kentucky, for decades, was considered prime training ground for racehorses because of the nearly year-round temperate climate and the quality of the soil, but Prock was of the opinion that Florida was the place to be. With our base of operations down south, he reasoned, we wouldn't need to ship our horses to a warmer location during the dead of winter.

Prock and I made a scouting trip down to Florida, and we hooked up with a fellow named Joe O'Farrell, who ran a fairly thriving farm called Ocala Stud in the center of the state. He and Prock were old friends. We toured the area, made various notes and so forth, and, at one point toward the end of our visit, O'Farrell said he was going to take us to the nicest piece of real estate in the region—a perfect spot, he said. "It's the best piece of land in the state," he gushed, "but you won't be able to buy it."

"Why not?" I asked. At this point, I was more than curious. Remember, I was a salesman at heart, and I was confident that I could negotiate myself into—or, *out of*—virtually any business situation.

"Let me show it to you first," he said.

It turned out that the farm was located directly across the street from Ocala Stud. It was called Greentree Stables. It was owned by Jock Whitney, noted philanthropist, sportsman, and one-time publisher of the *New York Herald Tribune*, and his sister, Joan Whitney Payson, owner of the New York Mets. Well, as I might have expected, the farm was spectacular and precisely what I was looking for: magnificent views, wide open spaces, excellent road access, and good proximity to local and regional airports. Really, in all respects, the place was perfect, and I didn't let it deter me that it was not for sale or that it was currently owned by such a prominent figure. The principal outpost of Greentree Stables was in Kentucky, and I learned the Ocala location was used primarily as a warm-weather haven for the younger horses. From the casual tour that one afternoon, the place didn't seem to be utilized at anything close to capacity. I figured it was worth a shot.

Prock thought I was a nut chasing after a fantasy, but I always held that it never hurt to make a telephone call. That next Monday, back in my office, I had my secretary place a cold call to Jock Whitney. Sure enough, the man got on the line straight-away, presumably following the flipside of my maxim: it never hurt to *take* a telephone call. I couldn't imagine that he had any idea who I was, but he was willing to talk to me just the same. So I got on the line and introduced myself. I told him I was the pres-ident and chief executive of the Alberto-Culver Company.

"And what does the Alberto-Culver company do?" he asked.

I told him and offered to send him some samples, and he seemed interested enough in the business, but I moved directly to the purpose of my call. "I saw your place in Ocala," I said, cut-ting right to it, "and I was wondering if I could persuade you to sell it."

"Buy it from me?" he said. "Just like that?"

"Just like that," I said.

"Well, it's not for sale," he said.

"I'm aware of that," I said, "but I thought I'd inquire just the same."

He seemed to think about this for a moment or two, and then he broke the silence: "Are you in the thoroughbred business?" he asked.

"Why, yes I am," I said proudly, and then I rattled off a few of our horses' recent accomplishments and purses. I mentioned some of the well-known jockeys who regularly rode our mounts. Clearly, Glen Hill Farms was no match for Greentree Stables, but we were just starting out and making a good name for ourselves, and there was no shame in that.

Then he asked, "And who is your trainer, if you don't mind my asking?"

"Willard Proctor."

"Ah, yes. He's a good man."

"He and I both agree that your land is just what we're look-ing for," I said.

And then, quite abruptly, almost as if I'd caught him at pre-cisely the right time to consider such an impulsive inquiry, Mr. Whitney asked if he could call me back shortly. I gave him my telephone number and told him I would anxiously await his return call, which he placed before the day was through. When he called back, he explained that his trainer was in the habit of sending their horses to the Greentree property in Akin, North Carolina, which, at that time, was another popular training ground for the horse set. Akin was a very sophisticated place, with an environment more befitting the wealthy horse crowd than an outpost town like Ocala, Florida. Really, at that time, there was nothing going on in Ocala, but there was something of a cultural community in Akin. This held some appeal to Mr. Whitney's trainer. "My trainer would like me to sell the Ocala place," he allowed. "He's a Princeton graduate, you know. There's not much for him to do in Ocala."

"Well, Ocala is just fine for me," I said. "How many acres do you have?"

He answered that he had three hundred and twenty-five acres, and then he named a price: five hundred dollars per acre.

"Okay," I said. "Sold."

Then he said, "Wait a second. It has to be all cash."

I said, "Okay."

Then he said, "I've got all this equipment on the farm I'll need to get rid of."

I said, "I'll take that too. Name your price."

Mr. Whitney named a reasonable sum and I agreed to it. Then he announced additional terms, and I agreed to these as well. We had a deal. Just like that. And all because I'd had the gumption to call and inquire in the first place.

To tell the truth, I would have agreed to a much stiffer price because I thought the place was a steal. In those days, it was probably worth twice that, perhaps even more. Walt Disney himself had just purchased hundreds of thousands of acres in nearby Orlando for his now-legendary "Florida project," which certainly wouldn't hurt the value of my small parcel. Just a few years later, in fact, when the region was being quite heavily developed, a builder offered me five thousand dollars an acre for the hundred

*The main entrance to Glen Hill Farms*

acres at the rear of the property, which I had not yet developed, but I wouldn't sell. The farm was too important to me and my family and a significant factor in the success of our thoroughbred business.

Bernice wasn't all that interested in fixing the place up at first, but I had it in mind that we might spend our Christmases

*The Bernick kids at Glen Hill Farms in 1993: Lizzie, Craig, and Peter*

there as a family. I should point out that Bernice never much
cared for Florida, but, until we found the spread in Ocala, her
idea of Florida was Miami Beach, Palm Beach, endless cocktail
parties, and one-upmanship. It wasn't for her. She never cared for
all that pomp and circumstance, the phony social swirl. We used
to go with the family out to Phoenix, Arizona, for Christmas and
New Year's, and it was quiet and understated and Bernice was
happy with that arrangement. But I thought that the farm would
be a nice change, so I had all the work done myself. I hired a
Chicago architect named Al Rosen and sent him down to Florida
with a Chicago crew. They made quick work of building a main
house, an absolutely stunning, predominately glass-walled design
that really is quite breathtaking. There was a small house on the
property to begin with, and we fixed that place up as well and
made it the manager's house. And, while we were at it, I had new
fencing put in around the entire property. I hired a decorator to
dress up the place with all the comforts of home. It was a Chicago

decorator named Christine Pertile, and she came in to show me all kinds of pictures and sample swatches. I picked out what I liked. Bernice wanted no part of it. Ocala was essentially a one-horse town, to borrow a worn expression that, in this case, didn't really apply in the literal sense, but I suppose I could understand her hesitation. After all, what would we do down there?

Nevertheless, I proceeded with the rebuilding and the redecorating and so forth, and before we knew it, we had an up-and-running horse farm. All accomplished at a breakneck pace, which, I imagine, was only fitting, given the nature of the thoroughbred business. I believe I toured the facility in early summer, and, by Christmas of that year, the decorator flew down with Bernice to lay in the linens, supplies, and finishing touches and to receive the three truckloads of furnishings that came in from Chicago. At this point, I'll allow, Bernice had done an about-face on the project, and she was quite charmed by the place and the possibilities. Over the years, she's discarded some of my decorating missteps in favor of furnishings matching her own taste, and that's been fine with me. I was just thrilled that she took to the place as quickly and as fondly as she did. And the children did, too. Really, the whole family fell in love with it, and, after that first Christmas in Ocala, we quit Phoenix for good.

Ocala was our home away from home from then on and the base of operations for our soon-to-be thriving racing farm.

<hr />

Now that we had our farm, it fell to us to stock it with promising horses, and Prock and I went on our version of a buying spree. We looked primarily to yearlings and looked ahead to when we might start racing. The West Coast was fast becoming a center of thoroughbred activity, and we decided to move our operation out there. The competition was good, the weather was excellent, and we thought it was a nice change of scenery for our racing team, to be sure, but also for Bernice and myself, since we were always on hand to cheer our horses on.

Very quickly, within our first few years on the West Coast, Glen Hill Farms began to dominate on the California soil. One filly, which I named Convenience, seemed the most promising of the bunch. In her first full season on the circuit, she tallied win after win at Santa Anita and Hollywood Park. Filly races, mare races—in nearly every race in which she ran, she was a factor. Hollywood Park was run by a fellow named Jimmy Stewart, no relation to the actor, and he promoted a race he called the Vanity, with a purse of one hundred thousand dollars. It was 1972, and with prize money like that, the Vanity became the championship contest of the season and was much anticipated by owners, jockeys, and racing fans. The race was open to mares and fillies—a mare, for those unfamiliar with horses, is at least five years old; a filly is younger—and Prock and I meant for Convenience to carry the day. Indeed, she went off as one of the heavy favorites, and, as it turned out, she won the race by about half of a length. She beat a mare named Typecast, who was also highly touted.

The entire Glen Hill Farms operation was naturally pleased with the outcome of the race; goodness, at that time, it was the single largest purse won by any of our horses, so how could we not be pleased? But it was over and done with, and the Vanity had come at the tail-end of the racing season, so Bernice and I packed our things, collected our family, and returned to Chicago, looking to return to our work and school schedules. Convenience was the champion filly, we all enjoyed a great season at the track, and that was that.

Or so we thought.

I don't think we were back in Chicago for more than an hour when I took a call from Jimmy Stewart. He was terribly excited, with news of some kind. "Leonard," he said, trying to collect himself, "Fletcher Jones thinks Typecast is a better horse than Convenience. He thinks the race should have gone his way. He wants to arrange a match race between your filly and his mare."

Fletcher Jones was the head of a California company called Computer Sciences, and, like me, he was relatively new to the horse-racing game. Before the vanity race, he had been somewhat boastful and outspoken about his horse and his chances, while we kept mostly silent and walked off with the championship. I could understand how he might feel that Convenience stole the crown from Typecast, but I wasn't about to subject our filly to a head-to-head contest. A match race was a rare thing in the thoroughbred business. Perhaps the most famous match race of all time took place in the late 1930s, between Seabiscuit and War Admiral—and, in many respects, it was bigger than any Super Bowl or World Series. More recently, a famous match race was run between Swaps and Nashua, and that also captured the country's attention. But I was never a fan of these head-to-head pairings. They were mostly spectacle, and often they had very little to do with determining a true champion. After all, the great champions all had to slog through the middle of the pack, jockey for position, and outmaneuver a wide field of opponents. A match race was an exhibition, nothing more. Oh, sure, a match race was exciting and it was a test, but it wasn't always clear to me what was being tested, so I wasn't much interested in putting Convenience on the line in this way. She'd won the vanity race, I thought. She was already champion. Let's just leave it at that.

"I don't know, Jimmy," I said. "I've never been a big fan of match races."

"Hear him out, Leonard," Jimmy insisted. "He wants to put up twenty-five thousand dollars, and he wants you to put up twenty-five thousand dollars. Winner take all."

I was, as you readers must now realize, something of a gambling man, but I had no interest in it. "Tell him thanks but no thanks," I instructed Jimmy. "Convenience is the champion and that's it."

The next day, Jimmy Stewart called again. "Fletcher is really upset," he reported. "He really wants this match race to come off.

He's willing to put up thirty-five thousand and make it a seventy-thousand-dollar race."

I still wasn't interested, and I said as much. Jimmy got off the phone to give the news to the Typecast camp. Meanwhile, I telephoned Prock out in California to bring him up to speed. I told him Mr. Jones was pushing for this match race and that it held no real appeal to me, but I wanted his thoughts on the matter just the same. Of course, the racing community is a fairly small one, so Prock knew all about it, and he had his own opinions.

"What about it, Prock?" I wondered. "If it were to come about, do you think we could win?"

"Oh, sure," he said, "but you have to make sure it's a fast track. She couldn't stand up at all in the mud."

Sure enough, Jimmy Stewart was back at me before the day was through with another offer, bringing the stakes up to fifty thousand dollars, but I still begged off. I wasn't negotiating or holding out for a bigger purse. I just wasn't interested. On his side, Jimmy was pushing hard for the race because it would be a big attraction for Hollywood Park. And Jimmy was a friend. I didn't want to appear unsportsmanlike, so I said, "I'll tell you what, Jimmy. Tell Mr. Jones we'll put up one hundred thousand, and he'll put up one hundred thousand, and if the track kicks in fifty thousand, that'll make two hundred fifty thousand. A quarter of a million dollars, Jimmy. That's one helluva match race."

"I don't know," Jimmy reasoned. "That's an awful lot of money. I don't think it'll fly."

"Look," I shot back, "I don't even want this goddamn thing. He's the one that keeps coming to me. If he wants the race, this is what it'll take. If he doesn't want it, then that's fine, too."

Jimmy called back a few hours later and said, "We've got a race."

I thought to myself, how about that? "When?" I asked.

"How does three weeks from Saturday sound?" Jimmy said.

I said that sounded fine, and the arrangements were made. I got off the phone and immediately called Prock, but news of the race was already in the air out in California. Really, it was a tremendously big deal in thoroughbred circles any time a match race of this magnitude came off, and I'd never heard Prock so excited. Mr. Jones let it be known that he was bringing in Willie Shoemaker to ride Typecast, which I thought was a brilliant stunt, but we were quite happy to have our regular jockey, Jerry Lambert, ride his regular mount.

Well, the weekend of the race rolled around on the calendar, and Bernice and I went out to California with Carol and my friend Dynamite Sokol, the well-connected fellow I wrote about earlier. We all checked into the Beverly Hills Hotel, which was where we always stayed when we were in the Los Angeles area. Scott went to college out there at the time, so he came up to the hotel to meet us. He had to get past a throng of reporters and media types, and he busted into our suite full of youthful brio and vinegar. He announced, "Jesus Christ, Dad, now you've gone and done it." He was caught in the swirl of excitement and frenzy surrounding the race, but, at the same time, he was worried the race wouldn't come out the way we wanted. Who knows, maybe he was anxious that I was frittering away his inheritance by putting up one hundred thousand dollars on a match race, but I think we were all confident that Convenience could pull it off— even Scott.

On Saturday morning, we all hopped into our car and rode out to the track, but by the time we got there, the gates were closed. It was noon, and the match race was scheduled for three in the afternoon, but the crowds had been piling in since ten o'clock that morning. There was a regular race card at the track, but the match race was the main event and the big draw. People had called me from all over the country looking for tickets, asking if they should put their money on Convenience, and wishing me luck, but here I was, about to be closed out of my own race! The security guard wouldn't let us past the gate!

At this, Bernice stepped from the car with her best take-no-prisoners demeanor and marched right up to the guard. "Sir," she said, quite firmly, "in case you don't know, there's a match race here today."

"I know, ma'am," he said, respectfully. "That's why this place is so crowded."

Then she pointed to the car. "That man in there?" she said, indicating me. "He's the man who's having the match race. You better let us through, or there won't be any race!"

Naturally, this poor security guard was no match for my feisty wife, so he opened the gate and motioned us past.

Our strategy was to go out in front and hold the lead the rest of the way. The race was a mile and an eighth on the dirt, the same as the vanity race, and the betting was fairly even going in. Convenience went off at four-to-five, and Typecast went off as the three-to-five favorite. There were nerve-racking moments as the horses were loaded in for the start because, in a match race, a good jump is key, and the horses weren't used to gearing up for a race without the hustle and bustle of an entire field. Convenience stormed out to an early lead just as Pinck and Jerry Lambert planned. As they took the first turn, I allowed myself the small satisfaction of thinking how smart I'd been to hire such good people to look after my horses. Lambert held the lead, but Shoemaker sat right behind us. Our lead held between a head and a half-length, but Convenience was never able to put the other horse away. Shoemaker and Typecast were always right there. I've got to tell you, it was a terribly exciting race, and I couldn't recall being more wound up at the track, more caught up by the drama of the moment.

Convenience came into the final turn and started to pull away, and my heart soared. She put a length, and then a length and a half, between herself and Typecast, but then, all of a sudden, Shoemaker darted to the inside and made his move. Typecast was a grand mare, and she still had some kick in her. She made to overtake Convenience on the home stretch. Our length became a half-length, and then a head, and finally the two horses were neck and neck. Typecast kept coming and coming, and Convenience couldn't hold her off. At one point, maybe twenty yards from the finish line, Typecast actually nosed out in front, and I thought to myself, aw, hell, we're finished. But we weren't finished! Convenience had some kick of her own; Jerry Lambert coaxed her to one final surge, and our filly sprang ahead and won the damn thing by a neck.

My goodness, I'd never been so excited! To have held the lead all along, given it back on the stretch, and reclaimed it at the last possible moment— it was a classic race, and I was thrilled that our horse came out on top. The crowd went wild, and Jimmy Stewart was over the moon. The last thing he wanted was for one of these horses to run away with the thing, and here he'd gotten a real battle, right down to the wire. I'm sure it was the best fifty thousand bucks he'd ever spent!

The actress Greer Garson was on hand to present the trophy down in the winner's circle, and there were all kinds of news cameras there, and all kinds of reporters. It was just a trumped-up match race, but it was treated with all the fanfare of a Triple Crown event, and I couldn't have been more delighted. Fletcher Jones was gracious in defeat, and there was no more talk of Typecast being the better horse. She was a fine horse, there was no denying it, but Convenience beat her twice—once on the track's terms and once on her owner's, so there were no bragging rights left for the mare.

Our filly had carried the day, and I carried home the biggest purse I'd yet seen in my still-nascent racing career.

Now, as anyone involved in racing knows too well, there are exciting pay days in the thoroughbred business, and then there are days you are certain that don't pay. Naturally, you remember the paydays more fondly than the nonpaying days, so those are the ones I choose to recall in these pages—not to boast, mind you, but to show how heady and crazy things can get at the track.

Actually, the Vanity generally has been lucky for me. One of our main jockeys over the years was the Hall of Fame rider Early Fires, who rode more than six thousand winners. Fires had a kid brother named Jackie, who used to ride for us as well when he was just starting out. As a bug boy, or apprentice rider, Jackie was entitled to a certain weight allowance every time he rode, the same as all bug boys. This weight allowance was extremely meaningful in a tight field. We had a horse at that time named Heavy Up, who happened to be a tremendous sprinter over six furlongs, but he'd never raced on the grass or at any greater distance. To Prock's thinking, though, the horse could manage the mile and an eighth just fine. Prock had the notion to enter Heavy Up in one of the other races on the day of the Hollywood Vanity the year following Convenience's win. He thought he might possibly sneak him in under the handicappers' radar. With Jackie Fires in the saddle and the extra weight allowance, the crafty Prock felt certain that Glen Hill Farms could ride home another winner.

Well, I had just under twenty thousand dollars coming to me from the window bets I'd made on one of our fillies, so I asked my son Scott to go down to the windows for me and place the entire amount on Heavy Up to win. I felt cocky and confident, and I trusted Prock's instincts on this one horse. Plus, I liked the odds. The horse had been spooked by a bird in his last preparatory (prep) race, so no one liked his chances. No one thought much of him at all. Heavy Up went from six-to-one odds to fifteen-to-one just before the race, and there's nothing like a long shot to get my competitive juices going. I normally wouldn't have placed such an excessive wager on such a speculative bet, but I was flush with the victory over Typecast. I guess those winnings were burning a hole in my pocket. Anyway, there it was, and our horse went off at twelve-to-one odds.

I must say, despite all the money involved, the race was not nearly as exciting as the match race had been. We led all the way and won going away by four or five lengths. It was a wonderful thing to see, but not nearly as wonderful as that nail-biter with Convenience. Still, I calculated my winnings in my head and figured on a windfall of about two hundred thirty thousand dollars— not bad for a day at the races.

This all happened on a Saturday when the banks were closed, and I didn't want to walk up to one of the windows to cash in tickets on such a huge sum. I needed to redeem these tickets at the track, so I sought out Jimmy Stewart and laid out my dilemma. "Jimmy," I said, "I've got a lot of money coming in, but I'd like to avoid a scene."

I showed him the tickets, and he did the math in his head the same as I had done. He knew a big payday when he saw one, and he knew how to take care of his good customers and his good friends. "When are you leaving for Chicago?" he asked.

"Tomorrow," I said. "One o'clock in the afternoon."

"Stop by the track at noon on the way to the airport," he said, "and I'll be here with the money."

Hollywood Park was closed on Sundays, which meant I could collect my winnings in relative privacy. I thanked Jimmy for his consideration and returned to the hotel. The next afternoon, I returned at the appointed time and Jimmy handed me a big shoebox stuffed with brand new hundred dollar bills. I handed him my tickets.

"Don't you want to count it?" he asked, when I tucked the shoebox under my arm.

"I trust you," I said. I thanked him again, and Bernice and I sped off. We had a plane to catch, and I suddenly felt very nervous about carting around a shoebox stuffed with cash.

Bernice and I were scheduled on an American Airlines flight that afternoon, and once we were safely seated on the plane, I tucked the shoebox on the floor between us and almost forgot about it. Halfway to Chicago, I got up to go the bathroom, and I wasn't but a few steps down the aisle before Bernice grabbed me and pulled me back to our seats.

"Where are you going?" she asked.

"To the restroom," I said.

She looked down at the floor, toward the shoebox. "You're not going to leave me here with this!" she said.

So, of course, I took the shoebox with me to the bathroom, and I couldn't shake thinking what a funny picture I must have made, barreling through the narrow aisles of that American Airlines flight, with my shoebox filled with money.

Happily, we made it home with our shoebox without incident—and a story to go with it.

---

The long-held dream for most owners in the thoroughbred business is to breed a champion. After all, it's one thing to seek out and claim a potential prize horse or to train a horse to realize its true potential, but it's quite another to start from scratch. Over the years at Glen Hill Farms, we raced dozens and dozens of champions. Truly, in virtually all respects, we were (and remain!) one of the top racing farms in the country. But each time I stepped into the winner's circle, part of me wondered what it would be like to celebrate the victory of one of our own. Don't get me wrong, each win was sweeter than the one before, and I was thrilled to have turned a lifelong passion into a profitable enterprise, but I looked on wistfully whenever one of my fellow owners took home the prize with a horse bred on his own soil.

But, good things come to those who wait, and, at Glen Hill Farms, we waited nearly thirty years on this score. Oh, we had our share of pure winners in those thirty years, but it took that long to get one of our homegrown champions into the winner's circle of a high stakes race of real national significance. Before I tell the story of one champion filly, however, I want to offer a few details on the horse racing game. As I wrote earlier, I had no real master plan for expanding our thoroughbred business; I simply figured I would take things day by day, opportunity by opportunity. The thoroughbreds were a passion of mine, to be sure, but I wasn't the sort to let my heart overrule my head, if

you understand what I mean. Each transaction, each decision
had to make sense from a business standpoint, and, under this
philosophy, it wasn't long before Glen Hill Farms was profitable.

I'll give an example. One year, early on, Willard Proctor and
I went down to the Keeneland Sales in Kentucky to look at some
fillies. We didn't intend to buy any colts because we figured we
could use a good filly or two to round out our stable. Well, Prock
told me about a colt named Relaunch that was up for sale. Prock
was familiar with the horse's history and told me what his line-
age was and so forth. Even as I found it interesting, I still did not
plan to bid on him. Still, we looked at the horse and studied his
gait—mostly out of appreciation for these fine animals. But we
were in the market for fillies, so most of our attention went elsewhere. When he came up for auction, however, there wasn't much
bidding interest, and as the bidding stalled in the mid-five figures,
I thought to myself, Leonard, it'd be a shame to see that wonderful animal go to another owner for such a pittance. Prock, I
could tell, was of the same opinion. Really, fifty thousand dollars
or so was nothing for a horse of such pedigree, so I got in on the
action—not in any kind of impulsive way, mind you, but with a
reasoned and reasonable head.

I threw a bid based on what Prock told me about Relaunch's
dam and sire. Sure enough, I managed to purchase the horse for
approximately sixty thousand dollars. It was a lot of money, there's
no question about it, but in the thoroughbred business, it was
also a steal.

The upshot of the story is that under Prock's steady hand,
Relaunch blossomed into a wonderful racehorse, notching any
number of impressive victories. When it came time either to continue his racing career or retire him to become a stallion, I sold
50 percent of him to another stable for two and one half million
dollars. Not a bad return on my investment, wouldn't you agree?
And he became a very, very fine stallion; we asked sixty thousand
dollars for his stud services every year for a number of years. He
died when he was nineteen years old, and, by that time, he had

become one of the soundest investments I ever made—in horses or elsewhere.

It used to be that the racing life of a horse was to six or eight years, and on rare occasions, it was as long as nine or ten years. Lately, with the breeding business in such high gear, many owners are enticed to retire their good horses with strong blood lines after their third or fourth year, particularly if they've had some success on the track. They're not about to take any chances, so they send them to stud. There's a stallion standing now on a farm in Kentucky, and his owners receive four hundred thousand dollars for his stud services. That's a lot of money, and it's just for one chance, with no guarantees. As long as your mare produces a live foal, it's a done deal. Still, despite the economics, some owners will run their horses into their fifth or sixth years. It all depends on where their interests lie.

Me, my interests have been all over the farm. I race. I sell. I breed. I'll even buy a share of a horse stabled to another owner if he or she has put together a syndicate or something like that. I'm in this business because I love it and because I love the possibilities of it, but I'm also in it to make a profit. At Glen Hill Farms, we've made our decisions based on each changing set of circumstances. There are no hard and fast rules on our farm beyond the simple rule that every decision must make sense on its own; there is no big picture, but there is an interwoven series of small pictures that together must make a profitable montage.

Another example is a filly we meant to race, but she turned out to be the most ornery animal any of us had ever seen. Our farm manager couldn't break her. Her name was Audit, and she was so mean and so strong that no matter how you approached her, she fought you off. There was no getting her to do what we wanted her to do, and so we determined to shift our focus and breed her as a two-year-old, which was a very unusual tact. But I felt we had no choice. We couldn't race her because she was so difficult to handle, and her bloodlines were strong, so Prock arranged to breed her to a racehorse he had once trained named

Maris. At that time, Maris was standing for a relatively small sum of money. And out of that came a horse named Uniformity, who became a very good big stakes winner for us out on the West Coast for a number of seasons. So, you see, even a carefully laid plan must sometimes be tossed out the window for another alternative.

As we grew, we had our racehorses all over the country running on different circuits in different seasons. Our grooms stayed with the horses at the various tracks, either in a tack room or right there in the stall with their charges. We moved our horses around for seasons or for specific stake races. We had favorite jockeys—Early Fires, Jerry Lambert, and Gary Stevens among them—and those fellows, in turn, had favorite mounts. Prock was a master at picking our best opportunities for our best horses. Always, we looked to move each horse up in class with each outing, but not too far up to so that it didn't have a reasonable chance of winning. And, if a horse was successful at one level, it was moved up to the next level as soon as possible. And so on.

Convenience, Uniformity, Afto, Tampa Trouble, Earn Your Stripes, Media Plan, Concept Win, Potentiality, Lonely Girl, Presentation, Header Card, Prize Spot . . . they were winners and good investments all, but more than that, they were all fine animals. At any time, I could walk through the stables where our horses were parked for a major race or for a season and look into the eyes of those well-bred athletes and feel a deep connection. They were my babies, all of them. I named them, I fed them, I bred them, I nurtured them. When I say *me*, of course, I'm referring to me and the rest of the extended Glen Hill Farms family, but the point here is that we all took it personally. It was a business, yes, and there were always bottom line considerations factored into our decisions, but beneath those bottom lines was an abiding love of the horses. And there's no way to put a price on that.

All of which takes me to the capper. The homegrown champion. A majestic filly named One Dreamer, by Relaunch out of Creativity. You didn't have to know too terribly much about horses to know this filly was special. You just had to look at her. She was graceful, fearless, and as powerful as all get out. She was quite responsive, too, her riders always reported. We ran her out in Santa Anita, and she won. We ran her down in Kentucky, and she won. We ran her at Belmont, and she won. It was 1994, and, by this time, Prock's son Tom did some of our training alongside his father. We all felt that this horse showed real promise, and so we decided to enter her in the Breeders Cup race, which was held at Churchill Downs, the site of the Kentucky Derby.

Now, most casual fans can name horse racing's three Triple Crown events—the Kentucky Derby, the Preakness, and the Belmont Stakes—and the truth of it is that we've never ridden home a winner in any of those bellwether contests. But it's also the truth that those grand races are shot through with excess and spectacle, and I've never felt it necessary to enter our horses in those crowded fields just for the sake of running them. But the Breeders Cup quickly emerged as the king of those high stakes races, with a big purse, a national television contract, and a top-drawer sponsorship arrangement with several major companies. Very often, some of the top farms forewent the Triple Crown circuit for a shot at the Breeders Cup, which, in its own way, became a rather prestigious upstart in the field.

And so we traveled down to Lexington with our entourage—including my grandsons!—and made all our last-minute preparations for One Dreamer's big race. As it happened, Early Fires was unable to ride for us that day, and this was a setback because Early knew the horse and her tendencies. He had ridden her to many victories to that point. But Gary Stevens was available, and he also knew the horse, so this setback was soon enough set aside. It's terribly important for a jockey to be familiar with a horse in a race such as this. He must know how the animal will respond in any situation, whether the horse will pull out or pull up, that sort of thing.

That year, the Alberto-Culver Company happened to be one of the sponsors of the Breeders Cup. As it turned out, we were the sponsors of the race One Dreamer was due to run, the Distaff, which was open to fillies and mares. The big favorite in the race was a horse named Heavenly Prize, which was owned by the Phipps family. The handicappers had One Dreamer down as an also-ran. I chalked up this assessment to the handicappers' shared ignorance and to our immense good fortune. I always felt that it never hurt to be the long shot—in horse racing as elsewhere—because it gave you the opportunity to sneak in under the radar. When nobody expects much of you, you can really surprise. Of course, it's only an advantage if you make the most of it; here our jockey, Gary Stevens, fairly snuck up on the field and rode a tremendous race. One Dreamer got out in front and led wire to wire, winning by about a neck. I must say, it was a special thrill to see our horse—our homegrown filly!—win in such convincing fashion. I'll admit that it wasn't nearly as exciting as that hyped match race out at Hollywood Park, with Convenience giving back the lead and reclaiming it at the very end, but in its own way it was exhilarating and enormously gratifying.

Bernice and I fairly careened to the winner's circle with our grandsons to celebrate with Tom Proctor and his crew. It truly was a heady, joyous moment. It was a million-dollar race, to be sure, but it wasn't just the money that overjoyed us. In fact, the money was the least of it. It was the validation, the satisfaction, the certain knowledge that we were doing something right. And there was also this: the moment gave me a precious exchange with my grandson Peter. He was eleven years old at the time, and I went against his mother's wishes and allowed him to place a small bet on the race. He bet twenty dollars across on One Dreamer, and, at such long odds, he was entitled to a considerable sum. If memory serves, he had about six or seven hundred dollars coming, which was a great deal of money for an eleven-year-old—certainly more money than he'd ever held in his little hands. He was positively over the moon with excitement, and I couldn't blame him. I thought back to my own boyhood miscalculation, when my friends and I pooled our meager resources on the "sure thing" of Shama Thrush but failed to account for the mud and the rain. I knew precisely what Peter felt. I was twelve or thirteen when I placed that bet, and I knew what such a windfall meant to Peter now.

Peter showed me his winning tickets. "Grandpa, look!" he said, with all the enthusiasm I might have shared with my own father, all those years ago. "Look at what I've won!"

I helped him to calculate his winnings, and he rolled the figure around in his head until I thought his eyes would pop out. "That's a lot of money, Grandpa," he said.

"It certainly is, Peter," I said. Glen Hill Farms had notched a seven-figure purse, but, in many ways, Peter's winnings were more significant. I flashed him a conspiratorial look and said, "Whatever you do, don't tell your mother about it." And then I smiled.

He smiled back, and, in that brief exchange, there was a line between the boy I was and the man I had become, a line that reached across three generations, connecting me to my grandson.

Sure enough, when we got off the plane in Chicago, Peter raced over to my daughter Carol and gave his mother a tremendous hug. Carol was there with a big crowd of friends and family to welcome us home, and as the back-slapping quieted, she took Peter aside. She said, "So, did you bet on the horse?" She wasn't angry, but she knew her son—and she knew her father.

"Yes, ma'am," he said.

"And how much did you win?" she asked.

He told her the amount, and she smiled. Carol's eyes sought out mine across the crowd, and she flashed me her own conspiratorial look, as if to say, "Nice try, Dad, but this is going in the bank."

And that's precisely where it went, the very next day, and when Peter told me about it all I could do was say, "I told you not to say anything to your mother."

# 9

# Success and Succession

YOU KNOW, IT'S A FUNNY THING HOW EACH ACHIEVEMENT TAKES YOU TO another opportunity, the way various successes, at various levels and in a variety of endeavors, change the stakes and your goals accordingly. You never know how a thing might turn out or where it might take you, and I suppose the only sure-fire recipe for success is to remain open to every possibility. Break it down, and you'll see that virtually every breakthrough—in business, technology, and beyond—has flowed in one way or another from a willingness to embrace a new idea.

Sometimes, new ideas are of a decidedly personal nature, and what this meant to me over the years was a constant redefinition of the business I worked so hard to create and a constant transformation of my role within it. For example, I never imagined that Bernice and I would build an enterprise of such sustaining value that it would outlast us, but it became apparent very early on that this was just what we faced with the Alberto-Culver Company. Initially, I merely wanted to create a business that could support our growing family and provide financial security for all of us; it was a one-year-to-the-next sort of thing. But as we moved forward and I redirected our profits and energies into expanding the business and outpacing our own performance and that of our competitors, I realized that our line of hair, beauty, household, and specialty products could very well thrive for generations to come.

And, indeed, it has. Over time, this presented me with a for-tuitous dilemma, but a dilemma just the same. After all, I couldn't very well micromanage every aspect of our business forever be-cause even an old fool could recognize that in doing so, I would run into the ground the very business Bernice and I had given wing. And yet, I also must confess, as our company eclipsed mile-stone after milestone—joining the ranks of Fortune 500 compa-nies in 1987, opening our one thousandth Sally store in 1991, surpassing one billion dollars in annual sales in 1992—the thought of one day handing over the reigns became something of anathema to me. Actually, *anathema* is perhaps too strong a word. Let's just say it weighed on me and kept me up some nights, this notion of stepping down from the day-to-day operations of our thriving business. One of the things that made the prospect so difficult to accept, I think, was the way Bernice and I ran Alberto-Culver as something of a family business. This was very much *our* baby. Sure, we were a publicly traded company answerable to shareholders, analysts, and regulatory agencies. On top of that, we had a network of more than five thousand employees world-wide. We were no mom-and-pop operation, that's for certain, but, at bottom, we were very much an old-school, my-way-or-the-high-way, top-heavy culture. We were closely held and tightly run. We did things a certain way at Alberto-Culver, and very often that way was my own. I shuddered to think how the place would function under anyone else. I came from a disciplined, hands-on, Navy background, which influenced the way our company was organ-ized. Bernice and I had our hands on everything, and we were fairly reluctant to give up that level of control. We certainly weren't about to give up that control to an outsider.

Happily, the outsider who eventually took over as president and chief executive officer in fiscal year 1995 had something of an *in*: he was Howard Bernick, a career-long Alberto-Culver em-ployee who rose through the ranks and proved himself invaluable. He was important to our family business sensibilities, and he was my son-in-law. In an earlier chapter, I recounted how Howard met

*Carol L. Bernick, Leonard and Bernice Lavin's daughter, president of Alberto-Culver Consumer Products Worldwide*

*Howard B. Bernick, husband of Carol Bernick and president and CEO, Alberto-Culver Company*

my daughter Carol and came to work at Alberto-Culver, but here I want to stress how Carol became a key component of our top management team.

From the moment Carol signed on to our shared enterprise, she left her stamp on virtually every aspect of our business, but, to my mind, her greatest contributions came in the area of new product development. That's really been her strength—that, and her ability to work with people and to integrate them into our bigger picture. In addition to her brainstorming of the market-leading Static Guard product, Carol also was instrumental in the development of several by-now familiar brands. In many ways, she brought our company out of the bathroom and into the kitchen.

Carol was the brains behind our Molly McButter product, an all-natural, butter-flavored alternative with no calories and no cholesterol. And she spearheaded the development of Mrs. Dash, the first herb and spice alternative to salt. In fact, as I write this, in the aftermath of the successful Winter Olympic games held in Salt Lake City, I am reminded of one of Carol's brilliant promotions to help introduce the Mrs. Dash item. At the time, in the early 1980s, there were all kinds of studies coming out in medical circles identifying salt as a negative contributor to a number of heart problems. So what did our Carol do? She arranged for Dr. Michael Debakey, the Houston-based coronary specialist who pioneered the heart bypass procedure, to join our team at the Great Salt Lake. We were handing out free samples of our new product, which we felt could replace salt as a seasoning in the preparation of many meals. And then, as a powerful symbol of the dangers of salt, the doctor accompanied Carol in the ceremonial dumping of tons of salt into the lake. Let me tell you, we got a lot of press attention that day—it was a photo opportunity worth more than a sixty-second spot on the Super Bowl!—and I mention it here for the way it illustrates Carol's attention to detail and her uncanny ability to call attention to our products.

Carol also engineered the very successful turnaround of our St. Ives acquisition and was the driving force behind integrating our latest products acquisition, Pro-Line International, one of the world's leading manufacturers and marketers of hair products for the African-American market.

In a different world, perhaps we might have looked to Carol to run our entire operation once Bernice and I were ready to step down. Goodness, she was more than capable. But as committed as she was to the Alberto-Culver family, she was doubly committed to her own family, and she wasn't willing to make the kind of personal sacrifice such a position demanded. She saw the difficult choices I had to make throughout her childhood, and she felt that she wanted to be the kind of mother who could attend a school conference at the last moment, drive a car pool, or be around to help with homework and fix dinner. I respected her feelings on this—I even admired her for them—but they left us short on the succession front. That is, until Howard surfaced as the likely man for the job.

Together, we envisioned a kind of partnership between Carol and Howard, with Carol responsible for our consumer products worldwide strategy the cultural initiatives that are so important. Howard would focus on the bottom line and the investment community. As we put our plan in place, Bernice and I felt mighty good about the future of the business. Howard would join Carol on the board, and when I was ready to step down, he would replace me as president and chief executive officer. I would stay on as chairman of the board, Bernice would remain as vice chairman, secretary, and treasurer, and Carol would assume her role as vice chairman, assistant secretary, and president of Alberto-Culver North America. It was, we all felt, a natural progression from one generation to the next.

And it would not have worked if it weren't for Carol and Howard. Really, Bernice and I liked Howard enormously, and we figured that anyone who could produce and raise such fine grand-children could be trusted with our family businesses. All kidding aside, he also brought a new vision to the company and an investment banking focus. I had no formal business education beyond seat-of-the-pants, but Howard looked to successful models admired by the investment banking community to build a new blueprint for how our company should function into the twenty-first century. I stood back, held my tongue, and watched him tweak our established practices in exciting new ways. One of his first great initiatives was the 1996 acquisition of St. Ives Laboratories, makers of a well-known line of shampoos, lotions, and other bath products. I must admit that I wasn't a big fan of the deal when it was discussed. I thought we were paying too much and getting too little in return, but I kept quiet about it. I figured that Carol and Howard knew what they were doing, and, in the long run, it turned out to be an enormously successful acquisition for us. I suppose the lesson is that it's never too late to teach an old dog some new tricks.

*Leonard and Bernice Lavin, 1999*

The other lesson—indeed, the abiding lesson—is that all good things must come to an end. Or, at least, to a shift in gears. We must all make allowances for age and the inevitable flipping of the pages of the calendar, only, in my case, I didn't see the need until relatively late into the game. Some people might see such unyielding determination as the product of a stubborn nature or an arrogant streak, but I choose to look at it as a matter of pride. I built the business without a penny of my own money and precious little debt, and now that we were a billion-dollar enterprise, I wasn't about to step aside before I was good and ready to do so. And I'd never be good and ready to do so until and unless we found someone to carry on in my name. Once we found that two-headed someone in my daughter and son-in-law, I allowed myself to get to that place in my thinking where it was time to slow down.

I was seventy-three years old when I finally stepped aside as president and chief executive officer. Of course, in stepping aside, I in no way retired. I still go to the office every day. I still walk the plant and offices, check on accounts and so forth, and often offer my unsolicited advice. I still have my hands in our ever-changing,

*Mrs. Lavin and children at the Bernice Lavin Childcare Center, Northwestern Memorial Hospital, Chicago*

ever-growing business. The only change, really, is that there're now two people in place to take the heat, make the final decisions, and close up shop at the end of the day.

Bernice and I are still involved—according to some folks, we're *too* involved!—but we're no longer consumed by the business, and that's a big distinction. We're no longer out in front. We give ourselves the time we need to take care of ourselves, to travel, thoroughly to enjoy our grandchildren, our friends, our horses, and our assorted other interests. Throughout our careers, we've both been active in the Chicago philanthropic community, and over the past several years, we've been able to give our time as well as our money to several causes and institutions, serving on hospital and charitable boards and so forth. One of our proudest initiatives has been the Bernice E. Lavin Jumpstart Fund, which provides seed money grants for innovative programs, typically in the areas of children's issues, health care and rehabilitation, and women's issues in the workplace.

Mostly, though, we now also have the time to look over our shoulders and marvel at the corporate giant we built from the fifty-gallon mixing drums of a lone entrepreneur. In marveling, I've come to appreciate my own version of the American dream. It's a dream that holds infinite possibility for those who work hard, think big, and keep an open mind. And it's a dream that lives on through my children and grandchildren—and the many thousands of Alberto-Culver employees and shareholders, who owe at least some piece of their good fortune to this same, shared dream.

Lately, my daughter Carol has taken to calling me "a living legend," and I always beg to differ. I may be living, but that's about where it ends. Yes, we've done some innovative things over the years; we've managed to build a business out of no business at all, to change the way we develop and sell common household items, but there's never been anything legendary about it. And there's no secret to it, either. The formula for my success can be the formula for yours as well. Determination. Pride. Vision. And, above all, a competitive streak that will never allow you to settle for second best because, as it says in the title, winners make it happen.

# Afterword

As I put the finishing touches on this volume, I realize that there are a great many people who helped me over the course of my long career. Naturally, my method of cherry picking stories to illustrate that career doesn't allow me to mention every last one of those people in these pages. Here, then, on the theory that one good turn deserves another, I would like to acknowledge some of the people who had a hand in making the Alberto-Culver Company such a long-running success. Each, in his or her own way, was instrumental to the growth of the company:

Dorothy Young, one of our first hires, who worked for us initially as an office manager and stayed with us until her retirement.

Bob Haag, who'd never been out of Brooklyn when I first met him, who signed on to the effort during our Stopette days, and who wound up becoming our national sales director and a significant shareholder.

Jack Egan, our southeastern regional sales manager, who, following our hard-won victory over the Teamsters during our union turmoil, was seen celebrating in the streets, hollering, "We beat the Teamsters! We beat the Teamsters!" His enthusiasm on this, and other matters, was infectious.

Arthur DeShon, West Coast regional manager, who once closed a deal with a buyer at one of the drug chains by spraying a can of our hairspray on the driver side "window" of his car to show how it alighted crystal clear, only to roll up the real window once the buyer exited the vehicle.

Grace Kaulfuss, eastern regional sales manager, who told a story about selling to a buyer for a key wholesaler on a hot, humid day in New York City, appearing as a cool vision of loveliness to the perspiring buyer. "Honey," the buyer reportedly told Grace, "whatever you want, you can have." As I recall, she came away with a great order.

Norman Kates, a regional manager in Philadelphia, who became the first Alberto-Culver employee sent overseas to establish an international operation in Great Britain.

Jack Soderling, southwestern regional manager, who moved up our ranks as general manager of our then-fledgling Canadian operation.

Chuck Walgreen, president of the famous chain that bears his family's name and father of Corky Walgreen. Chuck became a close friend and gave me a boost with my first product when I was just twenty-seven years old. From that moment, Walgreens has been a strong supporter of our products.

Also at Walgreens, there was Charles Mulaney, who offered us important support when we were trying to get established, and Bob Blaney, the key toiletries buyer, who eventually joined our company in promotion and sales.

Arthur Wirtz was a mentor to me consciously and sometimes without even being aware of it, from the company's earliest days. His son, Bill, has been a company director since 1978 and a dear friend.

Eileen Roth, a senior buyer at Thrifty, who gave us a tremendous assist in establishing our early products. As a thank-you, I saw to it that she received one hundred shares of our company stock when we went public in 1961, and, by the middle 1970s, that initial stake had grown to the point where she was able to purchase a retirement home in Palm Springs.

Maury Axelrod, vice president and general manager of the Thrifty drug chain and a long-time friend. Maury and his wife were fixtures at our Kentucky Derby gatherings over the years, and, unlike most of our guests, he always paid his own way to Lexington.

Dick Brown, chairman and chief executive of Sav-On Drugs, a major chain in the Los Angeles area. Dick and his wife also joined us at the Derby each year, and he also covered his own airfare.

Emery Larson, chief merchandise manager of Kmart and a years-long friend. Emery, too, was part of our regular Derby crowd, and a one-of-a-kind character. He made me a promise, on which, to this date, I have not been able to call. If I had a horse in the Derby, he said he would come, be the groom, and muck out the stall every day. I'm still waiting for Emery to do that.

Jack Schumacher, executive vice president of Wal-Mart, who also became a close friend. Jack was a top client of the Alberto-Culver Company, and he introduced me to Sam Walton, another fine man.

On the buying end, there was also Chuck Larsen, head of Cunningham Drug in Detroit; Hugh Crowson, top man at the wholesale drug operation McKesson and Robbins; and Walter Hause of Peoples Drug in Washington, D.C. The story with Walter was that he had some difficulty hearing, and I always had a devil of a time closing a deal with him. Sometimes, he'd flash me this blank look and smile, and I never knew where I stood. Once, soon after Bernice and I were married, we took a trip to Washington, and I said to Bernice, "Look, you go and see if you can sell this sonofagun." A few hours later, she came out to meet me, arm in arm with Walter, each one wearing a big smile. "Leonard," Walter said, "if you were as good a salesman as this young lady, I wouldn't have turned my hearing aid off as often as I did."

And, I can't leave off Murray Chaiken, head of the Sun-Ray Drug Company in Philadelphia, a man who was famous in our office for the way he tried to finagle every advantage in a deal. He was constantly jockeying to see how much money he could get out of the account for his promotional advertising, and so forth. For a time, they owned a radio station, and he tried to get me to buy time on it. Really, he just beat us right into the ground, but he was an important customer, so I kept up the relationship. One day, however, I went into a meeting with him with a fixed amount in my head, in terms of what we could handle on a deal. I told myself that I wouldn't let him wear me down. I had my figure, and I'd agree to it happily if I had to. Murray kept asking for this concession and that concession, and I agreed to it all. Finally, after about the fifth "okay," he turned to me and said, "What's with you today, Leonard?" I said, "What do you mean, Murray? I've just agreed to everything you've asked for." "That's just my point," he countered. "You're taking all the fun out of this game."

Walter Hyman, vice chairman of the First National Bank of Chicago, a very fine banker and a very fine man who helped me when I was first starting out in business for myself. On his retirement, we did most of our banking with George Champion at Chase Manhattan in New York, and he too proved invaluable.

Bart Cummings, chairman of Compton Advertising, and our account executive there, Peter Burns. Both men were extremely honest, considerate, and instrumental in launching our trademark brands.

Dan Seymour, chairman and chief executive of J. Walter Thompson, who came to see me in my office in Chicago one day and made such an impressive pitch for our business at a time when we were looking for new advertising that I gave him the account. I never regretted it.

Charlotte Beers, a brash, young Texan who worked as our account executive at J. Walter Thompson. Very smart. Very quick. Very talented. I tried to hire Charlotte to come work for us directly, but she was smarter than I was and went her own way.

Lee King, of Edward H. Weiss, a large Chicago advertising agency, who serviced our account for a period of years and was always very loyal, very dedicated, and endlessly creative. He's still a good friend.

At the television networks, there were Leonard Goldenson and Ozzie Tryez at ABC, Bob Kintner at NBC, and my distant cousin Bill Paley at CBS. I think the only time I didn't listen to Bill was when I declined to sponsor *The Beverly Hillbillies*, which became the top show in the country.

Ed Friedel, who signed on as comptroller of our sales company and wound up staying with me for more than twenty years. A solid, honest guy with tremendous dedication.

Dan Lewis, another close friend, who came aboard as regional West Coast sales manager for our professional division and did a wonderful job launching our Sally stores and serving as a sounding board.

Archie Bowe, a top Sears executive who approved the building of the Sears Tower in Chicago and who built up Allstate into an insurance powerhouse. Archie was a valuable member of our board of directors for a number of years, and, as he got older, he renounced all his board positions except the ones he held with us and Wrigley. I was always honored that he stayed.

Dick Ogilvie, one-time governor of Illinois and a strong contributor to the growth of our company as a respected member of our board.

My personal attorney, A.C. Lawrence, an exceptionally bright, honest individual, who served on our board with distinction for a long period.

Another lawyer, Jim Rhind, impressed me early on with his knowledge and insight into business and related matters. I tried to get him to join Alberto-Culver as house counsel, but he was also too smart for me. He ultimately became the chief managing partner of his law firm, and he has the honor each year of nominating the directors for our board.

Really, I could go on and on because one of the things I've noticed over the years is that no success is ever accomplished in a vacuum. I don't care what it is you're pursuing or in what field, but if you mean to do well, you'll need a helping hand every now and then. Indeed, as the title of this book states clearly, winners make it happen, but a true winner also knows to surround himself or herself with a team of supporting players to share in the effort and the rewards.

And so, to all those mentioned here and to those whom I will thank personally, you have my boundless gratitude.

Leonard H. Lavin
December, 2002

# Index

# About the Authors

**Leonard H. Lavin** is founder, chairman of the board, and chairman of the executive committee of the Alberto-Culver Company, an international Fortune 1000 company that produces and markets well-known consumer brands in the toiletry, household, and food fields, plus Sally Beauty Company, the largest distributor of professional beauty products. Under Mr. Lavin's direction, the Alberto-Culver Company became an international organization that manufactures worldwide, sells products in more than one hundred countries, and has annual sales of more than two billion dollars.

Mr. Lavin has won awards and honors for his philanthropic, civic, and business endeavors. Early in his career, he was presented with a gold medal as the International Marketing Man of the Year. In 1988, he was named Citizen of the Year by the City Club of Chicago and, the following year, was presented with the Marketing Statesman of the Year award by the Sales and Marketing Executives of Chicago. In 1990, he received the Steuart Henderson Britt award for Marketing Achievement from the American Marketing Association, and, in 1993, he was inducted into the Merchandising Executives Club Hall of Fame and the Junior Achievement Chicago Business Hall of Fame. In 1995, he was inducted into the Chicagoland Entrepreneurship Hall of Fame. By appointment of the governor of Illinois, Mr. Lavin was named Lincoln Laureate.

During World War II, Mr. Lavin served four years of sea duty and participated in nine invasions. Today, Mr. Lavin is actively involved in thoroughbred breeding with his farm, Glen Hill Farm.

**Daniel Paisner** is one of the busiest collaborators in publishing. He has helped to write dozens of bestselling and headline-making books with prominent entertainers, athletes, business leaders, and politicians, including Whoopi Goldberg, Anthony Quinn, Geraldo Rivera, New York Governor George Pataki, former New York Mayor Ed Koch, and FDNY Battalion Commander Richard Picciotto, whose account of his epic tour of duty on September 11, 2001, *Last Man Down*, became an international bestseller.